Japan

The Business Traveller's Handbook

Gorilla Guides
Travel handbooks for the business jungle

JAPAN

First American edition published in 2009 by
INTERLINK TRAVEL
An imprint of Interlink Publishing Group, Inc.
46 Crosby Street
Northampton, Massachusetts 01060
www.interlinkbooks.com

ISBN: 978-1-56656-775-6

Series originator: Max Scott
Series editor: Christopher Ind
Assistant editor: Charles Powell
Design: Nimbus Design
Photography: © JNTO/Nara Tourism Federation/Wakayama
   Prefecture
Cartography: Amber Sheers
Printing: Oriental Press, UAE

Opposite: The indigenous Japanese sika deer in Nara
Park are believed to be messengers of Shinto gods.

Japan

The Business Traveller's Handbook

Ian de Stains OBE

The Rainbow Bridge links the Odaiba recreational area to the centre of Tokyo.

The high-rise district of Shinjuku, one of Tokyo's many shopping and entertainment districts.

Mt Fuji is probably the most instantly recognizable image of Japan. At 3,776m/12,388ft the volcano is literally a sleeping giant.

Ryoanji Temple in Kyoto is famous for its rock garden.

Japan's high-speed "bullet train" the Shinkansen was introduced in time for the 1964 Tokyo Olympics.

The Great Buddha at Kamakura dates from 1252. It is the second largest Buddha image in Japan.

The Imperial Palace is home to Japan's Emperor and Empress.

Acknowledgements

Thank you choosing this book. There are so many out there.
But I believe this publisher's focus on the serious business traveller
is unique and I am thrilled to share my experience with you.

Guides such as this benefit greatly from the input of people in the
know and I have had tremendous help from a large number of such
people. They are far too many to mention individually and I hope
I will be forgiven for omitting the names of many colleagues and
acquaintances. However, I feel I must make special reference to
Ben Chesson and Simon Fisher of UKT&I and Catherine Taylor
of Austrade. My honourable friend Sukeyoshi Yamamoto OBE
gave a helpful perspective on the history overview and Akihiko
Fujita was invaluable in checking various data. Martyn Lee of
Discontent was most helpful in regard to robots. Jonathan Stuart-
Smith of Tohmatsu Tax Co helped clarify tax issues, at least to the
extent that my mathematically-challenged brain could grasp them.

At Stacey International I have benefited greatly from the
professionalism, patience and support of Christopher Ind and
Charles Powell. I thank them for their confidence in me.

As always I had the unstinting support of my PA in the British
Chamber, Sanae Samata, without whom I would never have
survived this long. Above all I am indebted to my partner, Hajime
Mori, who over more than two decades has helped me discover all
the wonders Japan has to offer and how to share them with others.

If this handbook does its job it will be in no small measure due to
all the help and advice I have received. I hope it goes without saying
that any errors or omissions are purely my own responsibility.

Ian de Stains OBE
October 2008

Left: The Torii gate of the Itsukushima Shrine in Hiroshima at high tide.

GRAND STYLE

DRAMATIC & INNOVATIVE

Welcome to GRAND HYATT TOKYO

FEEL THE HYATT TOUCH®

GRAND
HYATT
TOKYO ™
AT ROPPONGI HILLS

Contents

Foreword

Of all the major countries of the world, Japan is probably still the most mysterious and intriguing for travellers from Europe. Partly because of the language, partly because of the unique and complex national culture that has developed over thousands of years, Japan fascinates but also in some respects mystifies the Western observer. For 250 years, it was to all intents and purposes closed to the outside world (although it was never quite as closed as popular myth suggests). After being "opened up" by the US Navy and Western diplomats in the 1850s, and in the wake of the Meiji Restoration in 1868, Japan embarked on a process of industrial and political development at a speed and on a scale unparalleled in world history. The 20th century saw successively the disaster of the Second World War and the triumph of Japan's reinvention as one of the world's leading industrial powers and liberal democracies. It is an extraordinary history and Japan today is an extraordinary, complex and fascinating country.

Ian de Stains has lived in Japan for over 30 years, speaks fluent Japanese and knows this society well. As a businessman, and as the Executive Director of the British Chamber of Commerce in Japan for over 20 years, Ian is an expert in doing business in this difficult but rewarding market. But his insights into things Japanese go wider than business and industry. As an actor (in his former career) and as a writer and broadcaster, Ian understands Japanese society and culture in the widest sense. His guide will help both those new to Japan and those who know it well, but want to step back and think about Japan more objectively, understand this society better.

His book will also help those hoping to do business in Japan understand the demands of this very special market. He stresses the importance of human relationships; of taking time to understand the needs of Japanese customers and partners; of responding to the emphasis the Japanese place on partnership and long term commitment. Japan is a market that requires time, effort and patience. But it's also a market where the benefits and rewards can be considerable if the foreign company is prepared to invest that time and effort – as thousands of foreign firms have found over the years. At the same time, Ian's book introduces the novice to the niceties of Japanese etiquette (not nearly as complicated or scary as people think) and fills in the background, cultural and social, in a way that will help the traveller and the resident feel more at home in what can sometimes seem a very different society.

I have spent much of my diplomatic career working in or dealing with Japan, and I have had the pleasure of working with Ian and his colleagues in the Chamber for many years. I am delighted that Ian has written an up-to-date, accessible, and comprehensive guide for the 21st century on this important – but at a time of rapid global developments elsewhere, sometimes slightly neglected – country. Old-timers like me and newcomers alike will find it valuable.

David Warren CMG
British Ambassador to Tokyo
October 2008

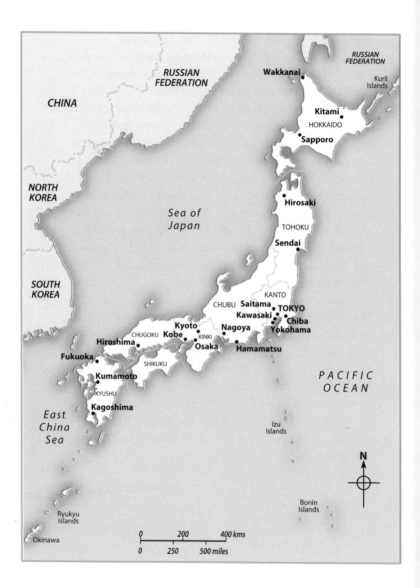

Japan

Japan yesterday and today

Japan yesterday and today

A bird's-eye view of the nation,
its history and the special features
that distinguish it from other countries

A condensed history

The modern country

Japan's geography & climate

Most Japanese people, when discussing their country
with a foreign visitor, will make the apologetic claim that
Japan is a small island nation. Yet the country is one and
a half times the size of the UK – roughly the equivalent
of California – and the thousands of islands that make
up its territory stretch from north to south in an arc of
almost 4,000 kilometres. In the northernmost regions
you'll find pack ice and ski-resorts; in the south, palm
trees and sub-tropical beaches.

More than 70% of Japan's land mass is mountainous –
indeed the archipelago is virtually split in two by a
chain of mountains – so it is little wonder that with a
population of some 128 million people, much of the
remaining 30% appears overcrowded. There are few
natural resources (though, with the recent steep rise in
oil prices, there has been renewed interest in Japan's
coal mines) so the country is dependent on imports for
the energy and raw materials it needs to sustain its
manufacturing capability. Though agriculture still
plays a hugely important role, Japan also needs to
import much of its foodstuff.

There are four main islands: Hokkaido in the north,
Honshu (the largest), Shikoku (the smallest) and Kyushu
in the South. That said, it may be useful to think of
Japan as three distinct areas. The upper third takes in
Hokkaido and the northernmost area of Honshu (known
as Tohoku) and is widely known for its agricultural and
dairy produce. The middle third includes the Chubu
region and the Kanto Plain, the most heavily populated
part of Japan and the country's political and economic
heart. This is where you will find the capital city, Tokyo,
and the country's largest port, Yokohama. Finally, the
southern third takes in the Kinki region (including the
cities of Osaka and Kobe – together the nation's second
commercial and industrial centre), the Chugoku, Shikoku
and Kyushu regions as well as the Ryukyu Islands, the
largest of which is Okinawa.

Geography

Japan as a whole straddles a number of tectonic plates
and is part of the so-called "Pacific Ring of Fire". It is
home to many volcanoes; the largest and most famous
being the spectacular Mt Fuji (3,776m/12,388ft) which,

contrary to popular belief, is not extinct, merely dormant. This geographical accommodation accounts for the existence of the many wonderfully relaxing hot-spring resorts around the country as well as the far from relaxing earthquakes that regularly shake the archipelago.

Quakes

Earthquakes are a fact of life in Japan. Literally thousands of them occur every year. The great majority of them go unfelt but many are strong enough to rattle nerves as well as windows and unfortunately, from time to time, some are severe enough to cause injury, death and damage. Tokyo and its surroundings were devastated by the so-called Great Kanto Earthquake (*Dai-Shinsai*) in 1923 when more than 100,000 people died, mostly in the ensuing fires. In January 1995, the beautiful city of Kobe was severely damaged in the Southern Hyogo Earthquake (*Hanshin-Awaji Dai-Shinsai*) when almost 6,000 people died and 100,000 houses were completely destroyed. More recently, in 2004 and 2007, Niigata Prefecture in the north of Honshu has been the site of strong and recurring activity, and on June 14th 2008, a magnitude 7.2 temblor centred in Iwate Prefecture caused extensive damage, injury and loss of life across a wide area of northern Honshu. The reassuring news is that seismic engineering technology is steadily advancing and it is now possible to build ever-more earthquake-resistant buildings, even to high-rise levels. The sobering reality is that predicting earthquakes is still an inexact science at best.

Internationally, earthquakes are commonly measured using the open-ended Richter scale which indicates the amount of energy the earthquake releases at its epicenter. This is expressed in term of magnitude (for example, the Great Kanto Earthquake registered Richter 7.9). Japan, while using the Richter scale, also has its own system of measurement known as the *Shindo* scale. This is not open-ended and ranges from Shindo 1 (unlikely to be felt by anyone who is moving around) to Shindo 7, which would indicate a severe and devastating earthquake. As a general rule 'quakes in the Shindo 2-3 range, while being possibly frightening, do little damage; Shindo 4 might see books and other items being shaken from shelves. At Shindo 5, objects begin to fall and it is difficult for people to stand up and at Shindo 6 windows begin to break and other structural damage is highly likely. (For advice on what to do if an earthquake occurs when you are in Japan, see Appendix 1.)

Given the reach of the Japanese islands it should come as no surprise that the climate is extremely varied: in the north, bitterly cold winters of Siberian severity and in the south, a temperate to sub-tropical clime. Japan as a whole, though, enjoys four distinct seasons and these play very strongly into the nation's culture, influencing such things as what clothes should be worn and what foods eaten.

The majority of business travellers will likely spend most of their time in Honshu where the spring (roughly early March through the end of May) is cool but comfortable. June brings with it the rainy season *(tsuyu)* when it not unusual to have several days of continuous rain; the wise traveller will carry an umbrella. July and August are hot and humid; there are often long periods with daytime levels in the high 30s Celsius and humidity of up to 70%. Although most public buildings and trans-portation systems are air-conditioned, this can make getting around the cities uncomfortable, especially if you are dressed for business rather than for the weather. In recent years – as summer temperatures have continued to rise – the Japanese government has introduced a concept they call "cool biz" encouraging businessmen to do away with neckties and sometimes even jackets. Autumn in Japan is arguably the most beautiful season, known for the spectacular colours of the mountain foliage. From September through mid-November, temperatures in Honshu's cities return again to very comfortable levels. But this is also the season for the typhoons that each year batter the Japanese islands. Roughly one third of the annual rainfall on the Pacific coast occurs during this season and the strong winds that accompany the rains can cause extensive damage. Typhoons are tracked very carefully by the Japanese Meteorological Agency and special radio and television alerts are made (many of them in English as well as in Japanese). Such typhoons often result in the closure of airports and Shinkansen ("bullet train") and other train runs and, at their worst, have people boarding up shop fronts and closing down businesses. Needless to say, umbrellas afford little protection from such conditions.

Weather

1

Winter in Honshu is typically dry and crisp with bright blue skies and temperatures rarely below 2-4 ○ C. February is often the coldest month. However, unlike in Tohoku and Hokkaido, it rarely snows and even when it does, it rarely lasts for long and the local authorities quickly have the situation under control.

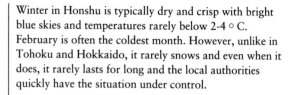

Japan's history – a brief overview
The early years

Most scholars of Japanese history begin with the **Jomon Period** (ca.10, 000 BC – ca.300 BC) distinguishing it from the preceding Paleolithic Period through the discovery of the pottery than gives the era its name. Evidence suggests that the Japanese of this time were hunter-gatherers. The **Yayoi Period** which followed (ca.300 BC to ca. AD 300) saw the introduction of iron use and wet-rice cultivation, ideas that were probably introduced from Korea. That country's influence continued to grow through the ensuing **Kofun Period** (300-536), during which the country was known as Yamato Japan and was centred on the province of Yamato (roughly where today we find Nara Prefecture). At this time the emperor's capital was frequently moved from city to city. By 552, Buddhism (another Korean influence) was firmly established. Encouraged by the ruling classes, it quickly found a place alongside Shintoism, the indigenous, animistic religion of the Japanese, with such figures as Prince Shotoku also promoting the import of ideas from China. Shotoku Taishi, as he was known, was regent for the Empress Suiko, and is credited with creating what is known as the Seventeen Article Constitution, designed to strengthen imperial authority. Then in the mid 7th century Fujiwara no Kamatari, a member of the powerful Nakatomi family began the era of the Fujiwara clan, whose influence was to remain until the rise of the samurai class in the 11th century, their power consolidated by a series of strategic intermarriages with the imperial family. During the **Asuka Period** (538-710) there were significant artistic developments, mostly influenced by Buddhism. It was during this period, too, that Shotoku compiled (in Chinese) the first histories of Japan, the Tennoki and Kokki.

Ancient History

In 710 Japan used the Chinese capital as the model for its first permanent capital, Nara. Large Buddhist monasteries were quickly established in the city and gained such powerful political clout that it was thought safer if the emperor and central government were to move. After a brief period in Nagaoka, the capital was established in Heian (today known as Kyoto) in 794. Remarkably, Kyoto would remain as Japan's capital city for more than ten centuries and it is why, along with Nara, it is held in such respect by today's Japanese and attracts such attention by visitors from overseas anxious to see some of this country's most splendid historical treasures.

Growing independence and power struggles

The **Nara** and **Heian Periods** (710-1192) of Japan's history saw the country develop a culture more independent of Chinese influences. For example, Japan had relied solely on Chinese characters (*kanji*) for its written language. Now, *kana* (an original Japanese way of writing syllables) was introduced and a new era of original Japanese literature became possible. The Fujiwara clan remained in control of Japanese politics throughout these years and their dominance was only ended in 1068 with the enthronement of a new emperor Go-Sanjo. His overt rule was somewhat short-lived but following his abdication in 1086, he continued to exert power from behind the scenes as what was known as the Insei Emperor.

The 12th century saw notoriously bitter power struggles between two aristocratic families: the Minamoto (known as Genji) and Taira (known as Heike) clans. After the Heiji Rising of 1159, Taira Kiyomori claimed victory and through the emperor ruled the country until 1178. After his death there was a further, and decisive, clan war (Gempei: 1180 – 1185) from which Minamoto Yorimoto emerged victorious. A ruthless man, he eliminated all his potential enemies – including members of his own family – and as Shogun, established a new government in his home town, Kamakura.

The **Kamakura Period** (1192-1333) marks a significant turning point in Japan's history for in the Kamakura bakufu it saw the first in a series of military governments that would rule Japan until the Meiji restoration of 1868. During this period Buddhism – which had been largely associated with the ruling classes – began to make significant inroads into the lives of ordinary people with the promotion of the tradition of Amida. Nichiren – founder of the sect named after him – also came to prominence and it is here too that the Zen tradition (with its stress on self-discipline and meditation) took root.

The second of the military regimes, the Muromachi bakufu, takes its name from the **Muromachi** district of Kyoto and this **Period** (1338-1573) saw the Shogunate expand its powers well beyond what had been achieved during the previous Kamakura Period, with the provincial constables of the time (*shugo*) adding civil powers to their military ones. However, it was a confused time with little consolidated power and for a period of some 50 years two power centres claimed to rule – the southern and northern courts. Imperial reunification was only re-established in 1392. It is significant that toward the end of the period (1542), two completely new influences found their way to Japan courtesy of Portuguese traders and Jesuit missionaries; respectively guns and gunpowder and Christianity. However, by the late 16th century the whole country was in turmoil with various warlords (daimyo) fighting for control. One of them – and reputedly one of the most brutal – was Oda Nobunaga. By over-throwing the Muromachi bakufu Nobunaga believed he could finally bring an end to a century of civil unrest.

There followed what is called the **Azuchi-Momoyama Period** (1573-1603) during which Nobunaga continued to eliminate anyone he perceived as an enemy, including a number of powerful Buddhist sects. In 1582 Nobunaga was assassinated but one of his generals, Toyotomi Hideyoshi quickly took control and in quick succession overthrew opposition in the north of the country as well as in Shikoku and Kyushu, finally reuniting Japan in 1590, the same year as he completed building his castle in Osaka, which still stands today. Hideyoshi's rule was marked by a stepping up of the persecution of Christian missionaries and he famously executed more than 25 Franciscans in Nagasaki as a warning to anyone contemplating conversion.

The persecution of Christians continued under Tokugawa Iyeyasu who came to power after Hideyoshi's death in 1598 and took total control of the country after the battle of Sekigahara in 1600. The emperor in Kyoto declared him Shogun and he set up his government in a little known village called Edo ("mouth of the estuary"). Today we know it as Tokyo.

Political stability

The **Edo Period** (1603-1868) was, finally, a time of political stability. The Tokugawa government wanted to be sure that no provincial daimyo would grow powerful enough to overthrow it and issued orders that all feudal lords should live in Edo for a certain number of months each alternate year. Furthermore, their families were obliged to reside permanently in Edo; effectively they were hostages. Secure in his seat, Tokugawa set about building his castle – the most impressive in Japan – and he surrounded it with a system of moats that radiated outward providing him with access to the sea and protecting the castle from enemy attack. Sections of the inner- and outer-moats still exist today, as does Edo Castle in the form of the Imperial Palace.

Edo Period

By 1788 the population of Edo was more than 1.2 million, making it one of the largest cities in the world. It was also highly developed in terms of city planning. Recycling was a feature of daily life: the tallow from spent candles was gathered to be melted down and reused by the chandler; hair was collected from barber shops to be fashioned into wigs. Even the night soil of the city's population was sold to farmers to use as manure.

Already in this era we see the strict division of Japanese society. At the top there were the samurai (the so-called warrior class retainers of the daimyo; those allowed to wear two swords). At the bottom were the merchants. In between were the farmers and craftsmen. And from the hands and minds of these latter came a great outpouring of creativity. In the theatre, *Kabuki* went from strength to strength and *Ukiyoe* (wood-block prints) began to appear everywhere. Production of porcelain, lacquer ware and elaborate silk brocades flourished as the city grew ever wealthier.

All of this happened, however, in splendid isolation. Tokugawa suspected that the opportunity for international trade might make other feudal lords rich and therefore present a threat to his rule. The Shogunate feared the influence of the West, especially Christianity. So in 1633 Japan closed its doors to the outside world. For the ensuing 200 years and more no foreigners were permitted to cross Japan's shores and no Japanese were allowed to leave. Anyone daring to defy this rule paid with their lives. There was a small exception; a colony of strictly supervised Chinese merchants in Nagasaki and a Dutch trading post on the small island of Hirado, both in Kyushu and far removed from Edo.

Ironically, the increasing wealth of the capital was in many ways the trigger for the collapse of the Tokugawa Shogunate. Once at the bottom of the pecking order, the merchant classes found that money had a power of its own; at the same time, the samurai began to face increasing penury; a sure receipe for civil dissatisfaction.

Yet it took pressure from outside of Japan (what today is termed *gaiatsu*) to finally bring the feudal era to an end. In 1853, the US Commodore Mathew Perry in his notorious black ships sat off Japan's coast demanding trading rights for the USA and after a stand-off, in 1854, the Shogunate finally gave in. The dam had been breached; the deluge was inevitable. By 1868, the Tokugawas had lost all vestiges of power and there was a return to imperial control under the Emperor Meiji.

Opening up to the world – and to democracy

The Emperor lost no time in establishing his court in Edo which he quickly renamed Tokyo (literally the "eastern capital") to distinguish it from the "western capital", Kyoto. **The Meiji Period** (1868 – 1911) was an astonishing time of change for Japan. From its long period of isolation the country emerged hungry for new ideas and ready for progress. The Emperor decreed that the samurai would no longer be permitted to wear swords, effectively emasculating them, and the daimyo were ordered to give up their lands. At the same time, civil liberties were improved and restrictions on religious observance were abolished. A European-style constitution was put in place and with it an election process that gave rise to the country's first true parliament (the Diet) complete with a Prime Minister (Hirobumi Itoh) and his cabinet, though the emperor still retained control.

In the comparatively short period that Meiji was on the Chrysanthemum Throne, Japan roared out of feudalism and into industrialisation at an astonishing pace. The Bank of Japan was created and the government encouraged the development of business and industry (textiles was a good example). It is here where the family-based industrial conglomerates, the zaibatsu, put down powerful roots.

Much of this progress was due to the influence of foreigners – architects and engineers, doctors and educators – who were invited to Japan to share their knowledge. By the end of the 19th century, more than 6,000 British experts had made a significant contribution to Japan's modernisation. British railway engineers built the first link between Tokyo's Shimbashi station and Yokohama, for example, and the architect Josiah Conder was commissioned by the then Foreign Minister, Kaoru Inoue, to design and build the Rokumeikan – a guest house and meeting place where Japanese could meet visiting foreigners. American, French and German specialists – though much fewer in number – played similarly important roles, and many Japanese traveled overseas to study. The nation's educational system was restructured, modelled on those of France and Germany. Change was everywhere, including in the way the Japanese saw their place in the world.

Nationalism began to rear its head. China and Japan had differing interests in Korea and this led to the Sino-Japanese War of 1894-95. Japan emerged victorious and in occupation of Taiwan but, compelled by the so-called Triple Intervention (Russia, Germany and France) to give up its other spoils, the Japanese military machine intensified and continued to increase its influence over Manchuria. It would not be long before differences between Russia and Japan (again over Korea) resulted in the Russo-Japanese War (1904-05) in which Japan was again victorious. The increased power Japan thus gained over Korea would lead in 1910 to the complete annexation of that country and sow the seeds of a discontent that many would argue is still unresolved today.

In 1912, the Emperor Meiji died and was succeeded by his son, Crown Prince Yoshihito, who in school had studied western subjects in addition to the more traditional eastern classics. This was perhaps fitting in an era which was to become increasingly democratic – indeed, some text books refer to the period as the "Taisho Democracy". But the new emperor was not in the best of health and by 1919 he was judged to be incapable of presiding over official ceremonies. He spent less and less time in the capital and more and more in remote imperial villas. Just three years later his son, Hirohito, returning from an unprecedented six-month tour of European nations, was declared Regent (*sessho*).

True power rested with the Diet and the newly emerging political parties and this led to reforms based on social democracy; labour unions and the rights of tenant farmers were recognised, for example, and there were the beginnings of greater equality for women. But the country's leaders inherited huge economic debts and an inability to adequately meet them. As if that were not enough, the Great Kanto Earthquake of 1923 brought economic devastation as well as human suffering on a massive scale. Whereas the Meiji Period had seemed full of optimism, the **Taisho Period** (1912-26) was anything but.

During the First World War Japan played a small role on the side of the Allied Powers, principally in confronting and defeating German colonial forces in East Asia. An apparent victor in the conflict, Japan was bitterly disappointed that at the Paris Peace Conference of 1919 its proposal of an amendment to the League of Nations covenant was rejected on what it believed to be blatantly racist grounds. The belief that Japan was being discriminated against was reinforced when the US prohibited further Japanese immigration in 1924. As the Taisho Emperor lay dying, the bright future that had been Meiji's legacy looked like being overshadowed. And so it proved to be. Given all that was to follow his accession to the throne, it is deeply ironic that Hirohito chose to name his reign Showa, which translates as "Enlightened Peace".

The path to war

The **Showa Period** (1926–1989) was marked by a growth in intense militarism, the dawn of atomic warfare, the renunciation of imperial divinity, and Japan's phoenix-like rise from the ashes of destruction to the world's second-largest economy – by far. It is also – to date – the longest reign of any Japanese emperor, beginning when Hirohito was just 25 years old and ending with his death at the age of 88.

The economic difficulties Japan had faced during Taisho continued and were exacerbated by the world wide depression of 1929. Domestically there was great unrest with regular assassinations and acts of terrorism. Communists became the target of persecution and censorship of the media and in education became the norm. During the 1930s almost all the important offices of state – including that of Prime Minister – were held by officers of the army and navy. Throughout, the emperor refrained from interfering, adhering to his role as constitutional monarch.

In 1931 Chinese nationalists began seriously to challenge Japan's influence in Manchuria which had been growing steadily since the Russo-Japanese war of 1904-05. The following year "Manchukuo" (a Manchuria occupied by the Japanese Kwantung Army) was declared to be an independent state and Japan also quelled anti-Japanese uprisings in Shanghai. As a consequence of these actions, the country was severely censured in the League of Nations, prompting it to withdraw from the world body.

Then in 1937 a relatively minor incident was inflamed by the Kwantung Army's over-reaction to it, prompting a second Sino-Japanese War, during which the occupiers committed appalling atrocities, especially during the offensive that would earn infamy as the "Rape of Nanking". The Chinese were severely damaged and heavily out-maneuvered but they did not give up and fighting continued – albeit at a low level – until 1945. Debate over Japan's role in China during this period and its need to atone for the alleged atrocities still goes on today and there are issues over whether or not the history text-books Japanese children use are accurate in their accounts of the period; the education ministry still has the right of censure.

In 1940 Japan secured an agreement with the Vichy Government of France to occupy what we know today as Vietnam and aligned itself with the German-Italian Axis. Unsurprisingly this put the country at odds with America and Britain who reacted with an oil embargo. Japan's subsequent decision to seize the oil-rich Indonesia (then the Dutch East Indies) meant that war with her former allies was inevitable.

The trigger was Japan's surprise and devastating attack on Pearl Harbour in 1941. There were, of course, other attacks in other areas and Japan took control of large territories from India to New Guinea. But then in June 1942, the tide turned at the Battle of Midway, after which the Allied forces slowly began to reclaim their losses. In 1944, Japan began to reel under intense bombardments – cities such as Tokyo were carpet-bombed – and a year later the Japanese island of Okinawa was invaded by American forces.

By 1945 the Japanese were being pressed to surrender but, whatever the diplomatic considerations, the military powers had no such appetite. So in Washington DC the decision was taken to use a previously untested force: the atomic bomb. On August 6th the inappropriately named Enola Gay dropped its payload – a single bomb – on the city of Hiroshima, resulting in an unprecedented amount of death and destruction that would have echoes long into the future. Not content with that, the Americans dropped a second such bomb on Nagasaki just three days later.

That month the emperor decided directly to intervene in the political process and announced his personal decision to accept the Allies' demands for an unconditional surrender as set out in the Potsdam Declaration. The war in the Pacific was over.

Occupation

Japan was utterly defeated. National pride was in tatters, its people were humiliated (the majority of them were also starving) and the infrastructure of its major population centres had been razed to the ground. On January 1st 1946, the emperor publicly renounced the divinity granted him under the old constitution, delivering an extraordinary blow to the nationalist elements and bewildering the majority of ordinary people who until then had revered him to the extent that they were not even permitted to look at him.

For the next several years, Japan would be occupied by the Allied Powers led by the United States but with the involvement of forces from Australia, Britain, India, and New Zealand. The Supreme Commander of the Allied Powers, appointed by the US President Harry Truman, was General Douglas MacArthur.

While the war was still being fought, plans had been made by the Allies to divide Japan up among themselves (as was done in Germany) but by war's end this plan had been scrapped, possibly because Truman feared increasing Soviet expansionism in Asia. SCAP had direct control. By August 30th MacArthur was in Tokyo, headquartered in the Dai-Ichi building – a mere stone's throw from the Imperial Palace – and by the end of that year some 350,000 US troops were stationed throughout Japan. The formal instrument of surrender was signed aboard the US Missouri on September 2nd 1946.

MacArthur proved to be generous in victory. On his arrival in Japan he immediately issued orders that no Allied personnel were to assault the Japanese people, nor were they to eat what scarce Japanese food was available. He also instigated a food distribution network at an estimated cost of some US$1 million a day. The General was also astute in his assessment of how the emperor should be treated. There is a famous photograph of the two, taken in September; MacArthur, in regular uniform but without a neck-tie, towers over Hirohito who is in strictly formal dress. Among the Allies, many called for the emperor to be tried as a war criminal and even on the Japanese side many – including some of the Imperial Princes – called for his abdication.

MacArthur resisted such appeals, recognising that such a prosecution would be a blow too far for a people already deeply humiliated; for all he had renounced his divinity, Hirohito was still a powerful figure and far more use to MacArthur as an ally than as a prisoner.

The purge

Military Tribunals under the occupation forces did, however, go ahead and many people were sentenced to death or imprisonment. Additionally, in keeping with paragraph six of the Potsdam Declaration, hundreds of thousands of individuals, from the military, in government and in business, were stripped of all their authority and the activities of various political parties, societies and other associations were prohibited. SCAP also removed Prime Minister-elect Ichiro Hatoyama and replaced him with the president of the Japan Liberal Party, Shigeru Yoshida. (For a list of Japan's post-war Prime Ministers see the box). In that same year (1946) a new constitution was announced containing what would become a most controversial piece of legislation, Article 9, forever renouncing war as an instrument of national policy. Other measures abolished the nobility, permitted women to vote and made significant changes in Japan's family law. The emperor was excluded from politics, becoming the nation's symbolic head, and Shinto was abolished as the state religion. The introduction of a Labour Union Law and a Labour Standards Law resulted in markedly improved working conditions for those in industry and a government plan to redistribute land gave millions of people who had worked for powerful landlords the chance to farm for themselves. SCAP's plan to help rebuild Japan's shattered economy appeared to be firmly on track.

Ironically, as the occupation neared its end, the USA's involvement in another war – in Korea – was a significant stimulus to Japan's newly developing post-war economy through a series of special procurements of goods and services to support the war effort. At the same time, with Washington's attention increasingly on North Korea's invasion of the South, it was logical that more power was given to Japan's native rulers. In 1949 MacArthur authorized sweeping changes that had just that effect.

SCAP

Two years later, in San Francisco, the signing of a peace treaty brought the occupation to a close. The San Francisco Peace Treaty went into effect on April 28th 1952 and Japan – for the most part – became an independent state once more. The exceptions, Iwo Jima and Okinawa were returned to Japan in 1968 and 1972 respectively.

Today, large numbers of US military personnel remain in Japan but they do so at the invitation of the Japanese government under a Treaty of Mutual Cooperation and Security. That is not to say that their presence is universally liked by the Japanese people, nor that Washington would not like to see Japan paying more for its security and even taking a greater role in it. Despite Article 9, Japan has one of the world's largest military forces – the so-called "Self Defence Forces" established in 1954 – on land, sea and in the air. The controlling Self Defence Agency controversially became the Ministry of Defence in 2007 and Japanese troops have recently been deployed (albeit in non-combative roles) in various conflict zones.

Rebuilding the nation

Japan's recovery from the devastation of war was rapid and remarkable. There can be little doubt that in the early stages this was in great part due to the continued influence of the United States. They were fighting a war in Korea and needed bases and supplies, and there was grave concern in Washington about the possible spread of communism throughout South East Asia; Japan was strategically important to all they wanted to achieve and everything they wanted to avoid. At the same time the Japanese government adopted a policy of giving "administrative guidance" to the nation's industrialists, identifying which industries would best benefit the nation and encouraging Japan's industrial development overseas. The powerful Ministry of International Trade and Industry – now known as METI – drove the agenda and many would say also contrived to put obstacles in the way of foreign companies wishing to compete with domestic ones. Whatever the underlying reasons, it remains true that in the 20 years following the end of the Occupation, Japan averaged an annual growth rate of eight per cent.

METI

The Tokyo Olympics of 1964 are often cited as the moment when the world woke up to Japan's recovery. Kenzo Tange's futuristic stadia, the capital's elevated highway network and the high-speed bullet train are the period's most obvious icons. Soon, Japanese companies began putting down roots in other parts of the world – particularly during the 1970s in Europe and the USA – manufacturing automobiles and electronics especially, and dramatically contributing to the economies of the countries in which they invested as well as ensuring that the Japanese economy itself would become the second largest in the world in terms of GDP, a position it maintains today.

From the late 1960s Japan has posted a current account surplus every year with the exception of a short time following the first oil crisis of 1973. The second so-called "oil shock" of 1979 prompted Japan to begin looking away from its traditional heavy industries towards semi-conductors and other technology intensive opportunities. While exports continued to play a vital role in driving the nation's economy, the 1980s saw increasing signs of trade friction with Japan's major partners all of whom called for a more open domestic market.

The bubble

It was a sure sign of Japan's increasing clout in the sphere of international finance that the country was one of the signatories to the Plaza Accord of 1985 (the others were France, the then West Germany, the US and the UK). The agreement was an attempt to help the US economy emerge from a serious recession by depreciating the dollar especially against the yen and the Deutsche Mark. One immediate result was a sharp rise in the value of the Japanese currency; by 1988 the yen was worth three times what it had been in 1970. As a result Japan's exports became much less competitive. The government's response was to encourage domestic demand.

Stock prices rose, there was a move to invest more in real estate and a growing trend to then use such real estate as collateral in stock market speculation. By the end of the 1980s, the value of land prices in Tokyo had more than doubled (it was estimated at one point that the value the land occupied by the Imperial Palace was greater than that of the State of California) and the Nikkei had risen by 180%. But what goes up must come down and when the government intervened to try to contain the rapidly inflating bubble, stock prices tumbled. By the end of 1990 the Tokyo stock market had written off some 300 trillion yen (well over US$2 billion). Land prices, too, dropped steeply leaving many investors with seriously negative equity.

Post-bubble blues

Japan's post-bubble recession was exacerbated by an increase in the consumption tax (to five per cent from three, which even at that level had been deeply unpopular) and corporate bankruptcies on a large scale. Land prices continued to fall, lending policies were tightened, and the so-called "Asian crisis" led to falling exports and thus falling profits across most industrial sectors. Consumer spending declined steeply and by 1998 Japan was experiencing negative growth. The government pumped huge amounts of money into efforts to stave off further declines and promote recovery. There were large increases in spending on public projects and in 1999 the Bank of Japan announced a zero per-cent short-term interest rate in an effort to ease the money supply. Trillions of yen were used to shore up major banks on the brink of collapse.

Most economists agree that things reached their lowest point in 2002 when issues over non-performing loans in the banks were finally dealt with and they could return to business almost as normal. During the so-called "lost decade" a good deal of restructuring took place; many Japanese companies shed non-core operations and through a variety of means increased business efficiency. Unemployment (which had reached over five per cent in 2002) began to fall again and between 2003 and 2006 there were strong gains on the stock market. Also in 2006 the Bank of Japan ended its policy of monetary easing and interest rates began to rise, as did land prices in central urban areas. In early 2008, for example, Tokyo's major corporate landlords were arguing that rent increases of between twenty and thirty per cent were both justifiable and sustainable.

1

At the time of writing, Japan – as with other developed nations – is seeing volatility in the stock market and has serious concerns over rising oil prices. That said, the fundamentals of the domestic economy appear to be strong. However, one of the main issues facing Japan going forward is what effect an aging population will have on the economy. Today something like 20% of the population is 65 or older; by 2055 the number will be over 40%. The consequent contraction of the working (tax paying) population no doubt spells a challenge for the Japanese government. It may yet present an opportunity for enterprising foreign businesses.

Politics as usual?

If the story of Japan's post-war economy may be described as dynamic, the same cannot be said of its politics. Immediately following the end of the occupation there was considerable confusion. The numerous conservative forces in the liberal parties – all in disarray – decided to merge with the Japan Democratic Party to form the LDP – Jiyu-Minshuto – in 1955. The Liberal Democratic Party would remain in power until 1993, when Prime Minister Kiichi Miyazawa failed to see through effective political reforms. A new minority government headed by Morihiro Hosokawa took power and the country was given the opportunity to reform an electoral system that many felt was at best unfair and at worst corrupt. Indeed, one of the politicians most strongly identified with the LDP, the powerful Prime Minister Kakuei Tanaka – dubbed the "king maker" for his influence in dictating who should be in power – was implicated in the mid 1970s in the Lockheed bribery scandal and was even arrested and given a prison sentence. Though he may have the highest profile, he is by no means the only politician (of any party) to be seen as being tarnished by corruption.

LDP

Japan's Diet is bi-cameral. The lower house (Representatives) is elected every four years (or earlier if the house is dissolved for whatever reason) and the upper house (Councillors) goes to the polls every three years to elect 50% of its members. Japanese citizens aged 20 or more are entitled to vote and they exercise a complicated selection process that is part first-past-the-post and part proportional representation.

Since 1993 the government of Japan has been in the hands of coalitions with no one party strong enough to secure a majority. At the time of writing the LDP needs the support of the New Komeito Party to secure its majority. New Komeito (which translates roughly as "clean government") was originally the political wing of a Nichiren Buddhist organisation, Soka Gakkai, though it claims to have severed those ties some years ago.

Perhaps the most realistic opposition comes from the Democratic Party of Japan (Minshuto) while there are also in play minority parties such as the Japan Communist Party (Nihon Kyosanto) and the Social Democratic Party (Shakai Minshuto).

Political parties in Japan tend to be made up of several factions, each one headed by one of the more powerful politicians to whom others pledge loyalty. When it comes to votes on major issues and at election time, there is a good deal of horse-trading among the factions and the outcome can often depend on subtle (and sometimes not-so-subtle) pressure from the leaders.

It is notoriously difficult to predict the political future, especially as an outsider. What is sure, however, is that Japan faces a host of new challenges that will require skill and courage if the country is to maintain its position in the world. A rapidly ageing population, a declining birthrate, a falling tax base, a need to accept increased immigration as a reality, and an effort finally to do what needs to be done to make Japan genuinely attractive to the overseas investor are just a few issues that tomorrow's politicians must grapple with. Fortunately there is a new generation of younger politicians entering the Diet, many of whom do not belong to a political dynasty. Some of them have studied overseas, have a truly international outlook and speak languages other than Japanese. These are the men and women who will steer Japan through the next period of its history which, like those that have gone before, is sure to present not a few surprises and ample opportunity for those willing to take Japan seriously.

Japan's Post-War Prime Ministers

Name	Took Office	Left Office
Shigeru Yoshida	May 1946	May 1947
Tetsu Katayama	May 1947	March 1948
Hitoshi Ashia	March 1948	October 1948
Shigeru Yoshida	October 1948	December 1954
Ichiro Hatoyama	December 1954	December 1956
Tanzan Ishibashi	December 1956	February 1957
Nobusuke Kishi	February 1957	July 1960
Hayato Ikeda	July 1960	November 1964
Eisaku Sato	November 1964	July 1972
Kakuei Tanaka	July 1972	December 1974
Takeo Miki	December 1974	December 1976
Takeo Fukuda	December 1976	December 1978
Kasayoshi Ohira	December 1978	July 1980
Zenko Suzuki	July 1980	December 1982
Yasuhiro Nakasone	December 1982	November 1987
Noboru Takeshita	November 1987	June 1989
Sosuke Uno	June 1989	August 1989
Toshiki Kaifu	August 1989	November 1991
Kiichi Miyazawa	November 1991	August 1993
Morihiro Hosokawa	August 1993	April 1994
Tsutomu Hata	April 1994	June 1994
Toichi Murayama	June 1994	January 1996
Ryutaro Hashimoto	Janury 1996	July 1998
Keizo Obuchi	July 1998	April 2000
Yoshihiro Mori	April 2000	April 2001
Junichiro Koizumi	April 2001	September 2006
Shinzo Abe	September 2006	September 2007
Yasuo Fukuda	September 2007	September 2008
Taro Aso	September 2008	

2

before you
get there

before you get there

An outline of some of the
organisations which exist to
assist the exporter, along with
an assessment of their focus
and likely relevance

2

Japan as a potential market

Japan is the world's second largest economy by far – larger than all the rest of Asia (including China, for all the attention it is given) put together. The GDP of the southern island of Kyushu alone is greater than that of Canada. According to the Japan Institute for Policy and Training, the average monthly income in 2007 was ¥523,000 (roughly €3,400/US$4,800) and the Bank of Japan estimates that the average amount of financial assets per household is around ¥10.7 million (roughly €70,000/US$100,000).

Japan's population is well educated: 97.7% complete high school and 52.3% graduate from universities. The people are also well read; in 2005 the number of daily newspapers published was more than 70 million. Seven out of the top-ten selling newspapers in the world are Japanese and the morning edition of the world's largest broadsheet, the Yomiuri Shimbun, sells more than the combined number of the largest ten dailies in the USA. The number of weekly and monthly magazines and the subjects they cover is nothing short of staggering and book sales also remain strong. Figures released by the Research Institute for Publications suggest that in 2006, 755 million new book titles were published and almost 2,700 million magazines were sold. For a country with a population of fewer than 130 million people these are extraordinary figures.

Market information

So Japan is a large and sophisticated market. Consumers have money to spend but they are knowledgeable and discriminating; they demand quality in terms of product and service. It is hard to define quality; harder still to explain what the Japanese expect until you experience it. But think the absolute best you can do and then exceed it. Products fail to sell here and companies don't make the grade when they fail the quality test.

Contrary to what is often claimed by those who have perhaps not tried hard enough, there are no true barriers to foreign companies wanting to do business here. While it is true that there are some areas where more deregulation would be welcome, new-to-market foreign companies in reality face no more obstacles than do new-to-market domestic ones unless you factor in the

2

EBC

language element and even that can be overcome. Arguably, foreign entrants actually have more resources designed to help them succeed in the early stages of doing business. And foreign companies do succeed. The American Chamber of Commerce in Japan has more than 3,000 members and the EBC (the trade policy arm of the national European Chambers) claims slightly more than that. These levels of membership could not be sustained if the companies involved were not succeeding in the Japanese market. That is good news in and of itself. The even better news is that foreign companies overall still have a very small share of that marketplace so there is plenty room for more.

So what sells? Walk down the main shopping streets of any Japanese city and you will see European brand names on every block. Chanel, Prada, Versace, Paul Smith, Vivienne Westwood; the list goes on. The largest Louis Vuiton shop in the world is in Tokyo and it is only one of many in the city. Foreign automobiles no longer turn heads. Volkswagen is the best selling foreign marque, but BMW, Mercedes, Land Rover and Jaguar are not unfamiliar on the cities' streets. Meanwhile, at the true luxury end of this sector, Bentley, Rolls Royce, Masserati and Porsche have remained strong even during recent periods of economic uncertainty.

However, these are not the only foreign products that sell. It is often assumed that the UK is best known in Japan for Scotch whisky and Burberry raincoats and scarves. While these products do well and sales are certainly welcome, the reality is that two-thirds of Britain's exports to Japan are industrial. Specialty chemicals top the list of exports with automotive products a close second. Coals to Newcastle? Perhaps. But what about Dyson vacuum cleaners challenging a saturated domestic appliance market (and succeeding in it) with a product far more expensive than most domestic brands? Or sophisticated sound-mixing panels for film and television studios, not to mention the countless licenses for the technologies that enable virtually every Japanese-made mobile telephone and the software behind the best-selling computer games? And that is just a little of what the UK is doing in Japan. The opportunities are enormous and are simply not to be ignored.

2

Opportunity knocks

Japan's population is ageing rapidly and while this
presents the country with serious challenges over
pensions and taxation, it also creates still further
opportunities for those companies who have something
to market to these senior citizens – the so-called "Silver
Market". The Japanese generally live long lives. The
national average life expectancy for males is 77.71 and
for females 84.62. A large number of people can look
forward to a long period of retirement and very many of
those will be fit and comfortably off. They will rightly be
looking for goods and services that will enhance their
life-style whether that is in the area of leisure activity or
in domestic amenities. At the same time, the traditional
concept of an extended family, where elderly parents
lived with and were looked after by younger family
members is rapidly breaking down. There is a new
interest in such concepts as sheltered housing and
hospice care, stair-lifts and barrier-free homes. Once
again, what may at first appear to be a pressing problem
for Japanese society could present significant
opportunities for business both domestic and foreign.

Be prepared

So what if you would like to take advantage of such
opportunities? Nothing can prepare you better than a
visit to the market itself. But just turning up for a look-
see is not to be recommended. The wise business traveller
will take advantage of all that is available at home before
setting out on what can be an expensive and bewildering
experience. But properly planned, it can be both exciting
and rewarding.

Chambers of Commerce in overseas locations exist to
promote their nation's business and help their country's
businesspeople. Speak to anyone who manages such a
Chamber and you will hear countless stories of how
much time has been wasted and how many opportunities
lost by people arriving in-country having done little or
no homework. It ought to be obvious: before embarking
on a business trip overseas, it is essential to be as well
informed as possible about your destination. The further
away from home it is and the more different the business
culture, the more vital the pre-trip research. Whether it is

2

your first visit to Japan or one of a continuing series, it makes sense to get the latest information about current trends so that you can take advantage of them. And no, it is not OK to assume that because you're familiar with Hong Kong or Singapore or even Beijing, you'll be able to wing it in Japan. This is a unique business environment with particular challenges and extraordinary opportunities.

What follows are a few suggestion on resources that might help you prepare for your visit to Japan. They are not, of course, exhaustive but should allow you to form an overview.

Your national Chamber of Commerce in Japan most likely has a website that will have the most essential information (though many are naturally designed for the Members already there). A visit to the site may be very useful, and you can also take the opportunity to let the Chamber know of your visit and ask if a meeting might be possible. While Chamber staff are not necessarily experts on all aspects of doing business in the country where they're based, it's a fair bet that they have a good overall grasp of the central issues and they will also have the contacts you may need to get answers to your specific questions. You may also be able to attend a Chamber luncheon or other networking event where you will have the chance to meet with fellow nationals already living and working there. (See Appendix 1 for a list of foreign chambers in Japan.)

JETRO

The Japan External Trade Organisation (JETRO) started out life promoting exports of Japanese goods to overseas markets. These days it is more focused on encouraging foreign direct investment into Japan (Invest Japan) and on encouraging foreign business to explore the Japanese market. With 73 overseas offices in 54 countries, JETRO offers business support advice and consultancy and once you arrive in Japan – where they have 36 offices – can also offer free office space for a limited period of time. They have a very useful website at http://www.jetro.go.jp/ where you can find a good deal of helpful information.

Japan's embassies overseas should also be able to offer advice, particularly if you contact the Commercial Section.

Japanese embassies

Australia

Embassy of Japan
112 Empire Circuit
Yarralumia
Canberra SCT 2000
Tel: (61-1) 6273-3244
Fax: (61-2) 6273-1848

Consulate-General of Japan
Level 34, Colonial Centre
52 Martin Place
Sydney NSW 2000
Tel: (61-2) 9231-3455
Fax: (61-2) 9221-6157

Canada

Embassy of Japan
255 Sussex Drive
Ottawa
Ontario K1N 9E6
Tel: (1-613)241-8541
Fax: (1-613)241-2232

Consulate-General of Japan
600 rue de la Gauchetiere oust
Suite 2120
Montreal, Quebec
H3B 4LB
Tel: (1-514) 866-3429
Fax: (1-514) 395-6000

New Zealand

Embassy of Japan
Level 18 Majestic Centre
100 Willis Street
Wellington
Tel: (64-4) 473-1540
Fax: (64-4) 471-2951

Consulate-General of Japan
Level 12 ASB Bank Centre
135 Albert Street
Auckland

2

Tel: (64-9) 303-4106
Fax: (64-9) 377-7784

Embassy of Japan
101-104 Piccadilly
London W1J 7JT
Tel: (44-20)-7465-6500
Fax: (44-20)-7491-9348

Consulate-General of Japan
2 Melville Crescent
Edinburgh EH3 7HW
Tel: (44-131)-225-4777
Fax: (44-131)-225-4828

Embassy of Japan
2520 Massachusetts Avenue
NW Washington DC 20008-2869
Tel: (1-202)-238-6700
Fax: (1-202)-238-2187

Consulate-General of Japan
350 South Grand Avenue, Suite 1700
Los Angeles, California 90071
Tel: (1-213)-617-6700
Fax: (1-213)-617-6727

Consulate-General of Japan
299 Park Avenue
New York NY 10171
Tel: (1-212)-371-8222
Fax: (1-212)-319-6357

Help on home ground

There are other sources of assistance, too, depending on where you are starting from.

Australia

The immediate point of contact for Australians looking for advice is Austrade
(http://www.austrade.gov.au/Contact-Austrade/default.aspx) which offers an impressive range

of customised services, including help with identifying international partners, providing tailored industry intelligence and support in visiting potential buyers. Services extend to those companies who feel they are ready to start exporting as well as those experienced exporters who may be looking to expand into a new market such as Japan.

NDEP

There are a couple of programmes of special interest; the New Exporter Development Program (NEDP) is focused on the dos and don'ts of exporting generally, while the Export Market Development Grant (EMDG) is a source of potential financial support.

Austrade provides general information free of charge while specific tailored advice is provided based on a quote in advance. Fees are based on an hourly rate of AU$190 per hour.

According to Austrade's website its services to Australian companies include:

- Advice on how to prepare for export – including country and industry information, help identifying international partners and access to Austrade seminars and events.
- Advice and information on the New Exporter Development Program (NEDP) and eligibility criteria.
- Export capability assessment and export advice tailored to individual business needs – including advice on export planning, logistics, budgets, and payment and marketing strategies.
- Export Market Development Grants (EMDG) and information on export financing, including referrals to other government financial assistance programmes.

EMDG

- Selecting markets and market entry strategy – including help identifying the right international partners, tailored research on potential international markets and free trade agreements, understanding the needs of international buyers and advice on developing a market entry strategy for your product or service.
- Buyer/partner identification and selection –

2

including introductions to potential customers visiting Australia and searching overseas markets for relevant buyers/partners.

- Assistance in overseas markets including advice on local practices and culture, market challenges, help with translation and interpreting and logistical support.
- Proactive help in identifying new export opportunities, including introductions to potential buyers through Austrade's online database and extensive overseas networks.

Canada

Canadian companies seeking advice can visit the government website at: http://www.international.gc.ca/commerce/index.aspx. There you will find details of the Canadian Trade Commissioner Service. There are also offices in every Province in Canada which can provide help and information. Specifically, there are four areas of support. The first of these will help you decide if you are ready to export. If you are, the next step is to determine if you are internationally competitive and to decide on a target market. If that should be Japan, the service will help collect market and industry information and then help you build an appropriate strategy.

New Zealand

New Zealand Trade and Enterprise is the major resource. At the time of writing, their website was undergoing some reworking but was still functional: http://www.nzte.govt.nz/section/11753.aspx

United Kingdom

The UK businessperson seeking help and information about doing business in Japan is well catered for. Probably the best place to start is with UK Trade and Investment (www.uktradeinvest.gov.uk). UKTI is an international organisation with headquarters in London and Glasgow and a number of local offices in the nine English regions and the Devolved Administrations of Scotland, Wales and Northern Ireland. It has representatives in Embassies and Consulates all over the world.

2

When planning your business trip to Japan (especially for the first time) it is a good idea to speak to one of the many International Trade Advisors based in the UK. These are often associated with a local Chamber of Commerce or Business Link. You can find the one nearest to you by going onto the UKTI website and inputting your Post Code. A meeting with an ITA can help you decide whether you are indeed ready to export and whether what you have to offer is appropriate to – and competitive in – the Japanese market. You will also learn about the various support mechanisms (including financial assistance) that are designed to ensure you have the best possible chance of success in the market.

One of the tools at your disposal is OMIS – the Overseas Market Introduction Service. This scheme puts you in direct contact with people on the ground in Japan; people who are ideally placed to allow you access to the best country- and sector-specific advice. These are the people who will also be able to support you during your visit, setting up appointments with potential customers, agents or licensees. This scheme is often used in conjunction with the Trade Missions organised by UK Trade and Investment. It is also worth checking with the major Chambers of Commerce in the UK when they themselves are arranging missions. You do not always have to be a member of a Chamber to join one of them. Missions may be either sector-specific (eg fashion, electronics, automotive) or open to companies from a number of different sectors. An International Trade Advisor can help you decide which is more likely to work for your particular business, taking into account the timing of such missions and your own business needs.

OMIS

The Export Marketing Research Scheme (EMRS) is another important resource. This is administered on behalf of UKTI by the British Chambers of Commerce (www.britishchambers.org.uk). It is an excellent way to identify key intelligence on such things as market size and segmentation, the applicable regulations and legislation, trends, distribution channels, as well as competitor activity and performance. This is a subsidised service and it is encouraging to note that companies with fewer than 250 employees may be eligible for a grant of up to 50% of the agreed cost of such market research.

EMRS

2

Talking to other British people who have lived and worked in Japan is also a valuable way to prepare for a visit (especially if it is your first). By far the richest such source of contacts has to be the Japan Society (http://www.japansociety.org.uk/) whose director is Heidi Potter based in Swire House, London. Though not strictly speaking a business organisation, the Society maintains strong ties with the British Chamber of Commerce in Japan and many of its British members have had distinguished careers in either business or diplomacy (or indeed, both). Its Japanese members are also of course an enormous potential source of information, contacts and influence.

USA

The US Commerce Department has a useful website (http://trade.gov/index.asp) where there is a good deal of information on the States' International Trade Administration service. According to the site, the main purpose of the organisation is to create economic opportunity for American workers and businesses. To increase trade and investment, ITA helps US companies identify and enter foreign markets. It does so by educating potential exports or overseas investors about the specific market in which they are interested. While the US is a major overseas investor and exporter, ITA recognises that for small and medium sized enterprises especially, taking the first steps into the international arena can be quite a challenge. The US Commercial Service is the trade promotion arm of the US Department of Commerce's ITA. It has 108 offices located throughout the United States itself and 150 around the world, covering 96% of US export markets. Its Web-based services are provided through the US government's export portal, www.export.gov where you can find a US Export Assistance Centre nearest to where you live. Alternatively, you can call 1-800-872-8723.

It is also worth noting that many States have their own promotional offices in Japan and while their focus is often on encouraging Japanese investment into the US, some of these offices may also be able to help potential American exporters and investors. A visit to your home State's website should make clear whether or not it has a

2

Japanese presence. Finally, it can't be stressed enough that the American Chamber of Commerce in Japan is one of the most influential American Chambers in the world. A visit to the ACCJ website (www.accj.or.jp) before you leave home is probably an idea worth thinking about.

European Union

The EU is a close trading partner with Japan and there are a number of significant Euro-Japan initiatives. The Major Chambers of Commerce in the EU Member States are the most likely sources of contact rather than trying Brussels itself, although there are country desks within the trade directorates. Of particular interest to businesses looking to Japan is the EU Gateway to Japan Programme (http://www.eu-gateway.eu).

The Programme's focus is the organisation of sector-specific business missions that allow EU companies to develop a productive and collaborative relationship with their Japanese counterparts as well as to gain an excellent first-hand understanding of doing business in Japan. Advice and logistical support is provided before, during and after the mission and help is also available during meetings with potential business partners. Participants in the programme can also take advantage of a wide selection of customised services (for example the provision of a dedicated interpreter for the week of the mission). In certain circumstances generous financial assistance is also possible. Since 1994 more than 2,400 companies from EU Member States have taken part in a Gateway mission.

The current programme lasts until 2015 and the business sectors in focus are:

- Construction and Building Technologies
- Healthcare and Medical Technologies
- Environment and Energy-related Technologies
- Information and Communication Technologies
- Fashion Design
- Interior Design

2

You can see an example of how a typical week-long mission is structured by visiting http://www.eu-gateway.eu/go.php?nID=51

The trade policy arm of the national European Chambers of Commerce is the European Business Council (EBC) whose home page is http://www.ebc-jp.com/. The EBC consists of almost 30 industry sector-specific committees and access to them is normally through membership in one of the stakeholder Chambers. The Committees, working with the EBC policy director produces an annual White Paper which is now recognised in both Tokyo and Brussels as being a highly authoritative lobbying tool. It will also give you an unparalleled insight into the current conditions in your sector.

Other sources of information

There are any number of organisations that publish databases and other sources of information about Japan and its business environment. The Teikoku Databank is available at http://www.tdb.co.jp/english/index.html and is possibly the largest single source of economic data as well as corporate information.

Another popular and reliable source is the Economist Intelligence Unit (http://www.eiu.com/) which provides a constantly updated flow of analysis and forecasts on something like 200 countries (including Japan) and eight key industries. The country reports are especially well focused and, as you'd expect, very well written. The EIU also holds regular conferences and if you should see one with a Japan focus just prior to your visit, attending it would be a very good element of your preparation.

3

getting to Japan

getting to Japan

The various considerations
in arranging travel to Japan

Visas

As of February 2008, Japan had put in place agreements with 62 countries and regions with regard to visas (See the box). Nationals of these countries and regions holding valid passports are permitted short-term stays for such purposes as tourism and business trips without obtaining a visa. However, if your visit involves paid activities the waiver is not applicable. Also, should you wish to stay beyond the period stipulated, you will need to apply for a visa[1]. This should normally be done before entering Japan.

Health and insurance

There are no specific requirements for vaccinations or concerns over health issues in Japan where the tap water is perfectly safe to drink and the population is broadly healthy. In the winter, it is not uncommon to see people on trains and buses wearing paper face masks, either because they have a cold and don't want to spread it or because they want to avoid catching someone else's germs. Contrary to some tabloid claims, this is not a sign of a polluted atmosphere; indeed Japan's cities are generally considered to be amongst the least polluted in the world. In the high summer Tokyo is sometimes – though rarely – affected by a photochemical smog and from time to time when the weather conditions are "right" the city receives a dusting of yellow sand from the Gobi desert. If you are prone to asthma, it would be prudent in these circumstances to have with you a nebuliser.

It is important, however, to be careful about bringing into Japan any kind of medication. If your medicine is prescribed, you should carry a copy of the prescription with you. Some common over-the-counter products, such as nasal inhalers (e.g. Vicks) are prohibited because they contain substances that are banned under Japanese law. Though you will most likely not be arrested for carrying one, it will certainly be confiscated if it is discovered. It goes without saying that narcotics and stimulant drugs – even those that are treated leniently in certain European

---

[1] The different types of visa and application procedures are dealt with in Chapter 7

Countries/regions with visa waiver agreements with Japan

3

Country/region	Term of stay	Country/region	Term of stay
Asia			
Singapore	3 months or less	Brunei	14 days or less
Hong Kong	90 days or less	Republic of Korea	90 days or less
(BNO, SAR passport)			
Taiwan	90 days or less	Macau (SAR passport)	90 days or less
North America			
Canada	3 months or less	U.S.A	90 days or less
Latin America and Caribbean			
Mexico	6 months or less	Argentina	3 months or less
Bahamas	3 months or less	Chile	3 months or less
Costa Rica	3 months or less	Dominican Rep.	3 months or less
El Salvador	3 months or less	Guatemala	3 months or less
Honduras	3 months or less	Suriname	3 months or less
Uruguay	3 months or less	Barbados	90 days or less
Middle East			
Israel	3 months or less	Turkey	3 months or less
Oceania			
Australia	90 days or less	New Zealand	90 days or less
Africa			
Lesotho	3 months or less	Mauritius	3 months or less
Tunisia	3 months or less		
Europe			
Austria	6 months or less	Germany	6 months or less
Ireland	6 months or less	Liechtenstein	6 months or less
Switzerland	6 months or less	United Kingdom	6 months or less
Belgium	3 months or less	Croatia	3 months or less
Cyprus	3 months or less	Denmark	3 months or less
Finland	3 months or less	France	3 months or less
Greece	3 months or less	Iceland	3 months or less
Italy	3 months or less	Luxembourg	3 months or less
Macedonia	3 months or less	Malta	3 months or less
Netherlands	3 months or less	Norway	3 months or less
Portugal	3 months or less	San Marino	3 months or less
Slovenia	3 months or less	Spain	3 months or less
Sweden	3 months or less	Andorra	90 days or less
Bulgaria	90 days or less	Czech Rep.	90 days or less
Estonia	90 days or less	Hungary	90 days or less
Latvia	90 days or less	Lithuania	90 days or less
Monaco	90 days or less	Poland	90 days or less
Slovakia	90 days or less		

Source: Ministry of Foreign Affairs of Japan

Where the waiver of visa requirements is up to three months or 90 days, visitors are usually granted a temporary visitor status for the full period (15 days in the case of Brunei) on landing. However, where the agreement is for up to six months, the initial temporary visitor status will be granted for 90 days. Those wishing to stay beyond this initial period must visit an immigration office to apply for an extension.

countries – are a complete no-no. The penalties for attempting to bring into Japan even minute amounts of such substances are very severe and conditions in Japanese detention centres and prisons are extremely bleak. The Japanese authorities make no concessions for foreign nationals in this regard.

If you should be unfortunate enough to need medical attention while you are in Japan, you can count on getting first-rate attention, but you should ensure that you have the appropriate insurance since costs – for those outside the national insurance scheme – can be high. If your private (or corporate) insurance does not already cover you when travelling abroad, your travel agent should be able to assist in finding an appropriate policy. Travel purchased using certain credit cards sometimes includes health and accident insurance and you can also contact such providers as BUPA. If you are travelling outside of Tokyo, your hotel is probably best placed to help you find a doctor who can attend to your needs[2]. Tokyo hotels can also help of course, but there are a few alternatives that you can access by yourself.

Medical services in Tokyo

The Tokyo British Clinic
Daikanyama Y Bldg. 2F
2-13-7 Ebisu-Nishi
Shibuya-ku
Tokyo
150-0021
Tel: (03)5458-6099

---

[2] You can also call TELL (Tokyo English Life Line) a free and anonymous counseling and information service that maintains a database of doctors who speak English and other languages. (03) 5774-0992.

3

The founder and director of the Tokyo British Clinic is Dr Gabriel Symonds, a British General Practitioner who has served the foreign community in Tokyo since 1984. He established the Clinic in 1992 to provide foreign residents and visitors with the highest standards of medical care in the tradition of British General Practice.

The Tokyo Medical and Surgical Clinic
32 Shiba-koen Building, 2F
3-4-30 Shiba-koen, Minato-ku, Tokyo
105-0011
Tel: 03-3436-3028

The Tokyo Medical and Surgical Clinic was established in 1951 in close cooperation with some embassies as a private general and surgical practice for the international community in Tokyo. There are a number of resident physicians and the Clinic can call on a variety of specialists. In the same location there is an affiliated Dental Clinic and a Medical Dispensary.

Tokyo Midtown Clinic
Midtown Tower 6F,
Akasaka 9-7-1, Minato-ku,
Tokyo, 107-6206,
Tel: 03-5413-0080

This recently opened facility is Japan's first affiliation with John Hopkins Medicine International, the premier medical institution in the U.S. From the latest in health-care services based on modern-day needs to traditional treatment, a broad range of services is offered.

Flights to Japan[3]

From the UK there are four airlines that provide direct non-stop flights (roughly 12 hours) from London Heathrow (LHR) to Tokyo Narita (NRT):

- All Nippon Airways (www.anaskyweb.com/uk/e) operates a daily flight from Terminal 3

---

[3] A complete listing of airlines that serve Japan is given in Appendix 1.

3

- British Airways (www.britishairways.com) operates a daily flight from Terminal 5
- Japan Airlines (www.jal.co.jp/en/) operates a daily flight from Terminal 3 (JAL also has a daily flight to Kansai International Airport in Osaka)
- Virgin Atlantic Airways (www.virgin-atlantic.com/en) operates a daily flight from Terminal 3

Passengers flying Upper Class on Virgin Atlantic can take advantage of the airline's private limousine service, drive-through check-in, and express transit to the air-side lounge which offers – among other indulgences – a Jacuzzi. The limousine service is also available from Narita to your Tokyo hotel.

Airports

Japan has dozens of airports, most of which handle purely domestic travel which is busy, especially at peak times such as the so-called Golden Week holiday (April-May), Obon (mid-August) and the year end Oshogatsu (December 30 – January 5) when people leave the cities to return to their family homes.

The main international airports are in Tokyo, Osaka, Nagoya and Fukuoka. At most of these it is possible to arrange for the rental of a mobile telephone (don't assume the phone you use at home will work in Japan). If you are making your travel arrangements through an agent or one of the websites referred to below, you might be able to pre-order and pick up your cell phone without having to complete lengthy documentation on your arrival.

Similarly, you can arrange a car rental if you feel confident about driving on Japan's roads (the Japanese drive on the left as in the UK). However, if you intend to do this you must obtain an international driver's permit (in the UK see http://www.rac.co.uk). It is illegal to drive in Japan on a UK or other foreign driver's license and penalties for those caught doing so are severe. It is worth remembering, too, that in Japan there is zero tolerance of drinking and driving so if you've enjoyed the in-flight champagne it's better to let the train (or the bus) take the

3

strain! If your trip will essentially be in the cities, you might want to think twice about a car; the roads can be very congested, there are highway toll fees and parking space can be both difficult to find and expensive.

Tokyo

The capital city actually has two airports, the New Tokyo International Airport (usually now just referred to as Narita Airport) and Haneda Airport which is mainly used for domestic flights but also handles international charters and a limited (but growing) number of commercial international flights mostly to China and South Korea.

Narita airport is, in fact, not in Tokyo but in Chiba Prefecture, some 60 kilometres from the city. Access to Tokyo itself is by train (either the Narita Express to Tokyo, Ikebukuro or Shinjuku Stations, or the Keisei Skyliner to Ueno Station) or by limousine bus. There are also rail and road services to Yokohama.

The buses stop at a number of points in the city, including most of the major hotels. Depending on the traffic, the bus will take longer than the train. On the other hand, the busses run more frequently and there is the added advantage of being delivered to your hotel doorstep. The cost (roughly ¥3,000) is about the same for either service. But be warned: credit cards are not accepted. You will need to pay cash for your ticket into town.

Taxis are readily available but the fare into central Tokyo will be in the order of ¥25,000 (US$250/€185.) and possibly more if the traffic on the expressway is heavy which it frequently is.

Osaka

Osaka also has two airports. Confusingly, that which is known as Osaka International Airport now only handles domestic flights. The other, Kansai International Airport (KIX) is located on an artificial island in the middle of Osaka Bay. It is connected to the mainland by the Sky Gate Bridge R which carries road and rail services.

3

Nagoya

Nagoya's international airport (NGO) is known as Centrair – a contraction of Central Japan International Airport. It is well served by rail and bus services into the city and even a high-speed boat across Ise Bay to Mie Prefecture.

Fukuoka

The only international airport in Japan to be actually located in the city it is named for, Fukuoka (FUK) has a direct subway link to the city centre itself. It also has a domestic terminal making for quick and easy transfers.

Making your own way

If you are planning your own trip, a good travel agent can help save you time and money with appropriate recommendations for the best prices on flights and accommodation, including the special deals many of the leading hotels offer from time to time. They should also be able to arrange for a Japan Rail Pass and cell phone rental. The better ones may also help you with business cards, properly translated. (More on the importance of business cards in Chapter 4.)

It is, of course, possible to arrange everything by yourself, ensuring the utmost flexibility. Fortunately there are a number of very useful websites that you can turn to:

The Japan National Tourist Organisation has a multi-lingual site that is attractive and packed with useful information: www.jnto.go.jp/

Travel Japan is a bilingual site that allows you to book flights and accommodation, order Rail Passes, rent a cell phone and much more: www.japantravel.co.uk/site/default.html

Japan Guide.com is very similar in nature to Travel Japan and has proved useful in the preparation of this handbook: www.japan-guide.com/

3

Trade missions

If you are planning your first visit to Japan, it is worth considering a Trade Mission, where all the arrangements are taken care of, including setting up meetings, provision of interpreters and pre-visit orientation. Sometimes and in certain circumstances there are financial subsidies available to eligible participants. Missions may be organised on an industry-sector basis (automotive, fashion, pharmaceutical, software etc) or they may be more general and open to representatives of any industry.

In the UK you can get help in deciding which kind of mission might work best for you by consulting an International Trade Advisor in **UK Trade and Investment** (see Chapter 2 for more details). Additionally, several of the major Chambers of Commerce run regular missions and you do not always have to belong to the particular Chamber in order to take part. Meanwhile, the devolved administrations can also help companies operating in their territories.

The Scottish Council for Development and Industry (www.scdi.org.uk/) is an independent networking organisation that regularly organises trade missions, some of which offer financial aid.

International Business Wales (www.ibwales.com/) also runs trade missions.

In Northern Ireland, the **Department of Enterprise Trade and Investment** (www.detini.gov.uk/) offers advice on international trade and exporting to companies in the province.

One of the largest programmes offering trade missions is the **EU Gateway to Japan**, more details of which are given in Chapter 2.

4

both feet on
the ground

both feet
on the ground

This section takes the reader by
the hand and talks through the
nitty-gritty of everyday life.
Knowledge of these essentials
provides the confidence to go out
and do business effectively

The shelves of bookstores throughout the English speaking world groan with books about Japan; how to do business there, what it's like living there, its history, its culture, the martial arts. The list is seemingly endless. Some are scholarly, some tabloid in their approach. Some are written by people who've never even lived there, many by people who don't have sufficient grasp of the language to research at first hand. It is a measure of how fascinating the country and its culture are that so much effort goes into producing such books and an indication of just how complex a subject it is that none of them actually gets it one hundred percent right. Nor will this one. All an aspiring author can do is share what knowledge and insights he has and hope that they strike a chord with at least some readers, so that a business trip here is made that much less daunting and that much more enjoyable. Hopefully that will translate into a trip that is also productive. However, it would be unrealistic to expect that a first visit would yield much more than the successful building of relationships; clinching a deal and signing a contract first time out is practically unheard of. Which is not to say it is entirely impossible.

After all, Japan is full of contrasts and contradictions; that is one of the things that makes it so fascinating to many foreigners who choose to live here. But it can sometimes be frustrating. One thing that helps is to remember that, broadly speaking, the Japanese are comfortable with paradox. Whereas in the west we are taught that something is always either black or white, right or wrong, good or bad, that is not necessarily the case in Japan where opposites can – and do – co-exist quite comfortably. Allowing that just to be so, without trying to understand why or trying to make it fit your own paradigm goes a long way to dealing with a certain amount of culture shock (and, by the way, culture shock is not always a bad thing; it can help us see things differently, shake us out of complacency and even inspire new ideas).

It is easy to look around Tokyo and see it as just another large international city (which of course on many levels it is) but you really do not have to scratch the surface very deeply to realise that it is an Asian city and that its values

Research

4

4

are fundamentally Asian. The further you stray from the main urban centres, the clearer that becomes.

Japanese society by and large works as it does because of an adherence (whether consciously or not) to the basic Confucian values of respect for others, particularly respect for seniority, age and authority, and an avoidance of confrontation in favour of achieving consensus.

There are not the striking class or wealth differences that you find in many other societies[1]. People are respected for the work they do and so their self-respect is healthy. Consider the city's garbage collectors in their bright clean uniforms and finely polished garbage trucks. No-one looks down on them; they do an important job and they take pride in doing it well. Construction sites are shielded with clean tarpaulin and the entrances where the trucks come and go are regularly hosed down to still the dust and sweep away any debris. Buses and subway trains are spotless and well maintained. There is no litter in the streets and on station platforms[2]. In short, it is an orderly society where there is very little crime and where shame is a bigger motivating factor than guilt; to lose face is to lose all.

Some argue that it is also a society in which individual expression is suppressed, where creativity is lacking. There is something in that. With few exceptions Japan's education system from kindergarten to university does not teach pupils how to think, but what to think. Learning lessons by rote leads to the passing of exams and that is all that counts. Japan's finely developed management skills have been copied in many sectors and in many countries. But when it comes to leadership, Japan is simply not in the major league. Where is the Japanese Richard Branson; where Japan's Bill Gates? You could also apply the argument to Japanese political leadership, which would merit a book all to itself!

---

[1] There are some signs that wage differences are beginning to expand.
[2] One of the contradictions: Mt Fuji during climbing season becomes a huge rubbish dump.

There is an expression in Japanese that roughly translates as "the nail that stands up gets hammered down". The average Japanese is much more comfortable being part of a group than being the centre of attention. Collective, rather than individual, responsibility is the preferred choice. Understanding this explains – at least in part – why many business meetings involve so many people on the Japanese side (more on this in Chapter 5).

This handbook is not intended to be a cultural primer as such, but it may be helpful to bear these all-too-brief reflections in mind as you set about your trip.

4

Now to some practicalities:
Business Cards *(meishi)*
One of the most important tools in the businessman's arsenal, appropriate name cards are essential; without them you are literally a non-person. Meishi are your identity and your credibility. Decide on how many you think you might need and then triple the number; there is nothing more embarrassing than telling people you have run out of cards. Here are some other important points:

- The cards should be standard size (9.00 x 5.5 cm) so that they fit in the small case that everyone carries around and in the box file in the office. Non-standard sizes are inconvenient and send the wrong message about you;
- The cards should be bi-lingual, one side English, the other Japanese. Make sure the Japanese is translated correctly and that your name in *katakana*[3] is as close to the correct pronunciation of your name as possible;
- The cards should contain your company name and logo, your job title, your name and primary contact details. Don't be tempted to add unnecessary information;
- Photographs and other attempts to be creative are not to be encouraged;
- Use good quality white card and keep the printing clean and simple;

---

[3] The phonetic syllabry used to write foreign names and loan words

- Use a *meishi* holder (card case) to keep the cards looking new. Offering a dirty or ragged card is disrespectful and sends the wrong message.

Don't underestimate the importance attached to *meishi* and the proper way of handling them. More on *meishi* manners in Chapter 5.

4

Banking

For all Japan's efficiencies in many areas, the banking system is striking for its many inefficiencies (another one of those contradictions!). As a business traveller you will probably be spared the worst as you are most likely to need only the money exchange services. But here, too, be prepared to take a number and wait for the various processes that have to be gone through and wait some more while they are checked and double-checked. Don't assume that every branch of even the biggest banks will have a money exchange. It is usually only the larger and more centrally located ones that do. You can avoid the banks altogether if you exchange money/travellers checks at your hotel, but you will get a less favourable rate. Japan does not have the type of money exchange kiosks that you find in some European cities.

Japanese banking hours are 09.00 – 15.00 Monday to Friday with the exception of National Holidays (see Appendix-1). ATMs stay open after hours but some close at 17.00, others at 19.00; a few stay open 24 hours a day (especially those in the so-called "convenience stores". However, don't assume that you can use your bank card (check with your bank before you leave whether the card it issues will work in Japan). Some machines allow you to withdraw cash using a credit card.

The foreign exchange counters in the larger banks usually have English-speaking staff but if by chance you do have to transact something less straightforward than exchanging currencies, it is advisable to have a Japanese speaker on hand to help you.

As a visitor you cannot open a bank account in Japan. Foreign residents may do so on production of the Alien

Registration Card[4] that must be carried at all times. Foreign banks generally do not offer personal retail services. The exception is Citibank. In addition, Standard Chartered Bank and HSBC offer private banking for high net worth individuals and Lloyds TSB offers a system called Go Lloyds enabling foreign residents to remit money to the UK more easily and at cheaper rates than a Japanese bank.

Money

Japan's currency is the Yen. Notes come in 1,000, 2,000, 5,000 and 10,000 denominations. There are 1, 5, 10, 50, 100, and 500 coins.

Credit and pre-paid cards

Credit cards are more widely accepted now than they were even a few years ago, but not universally so, so it is wise to check before hand in restaurants (especially small ones). Some taxis will accept credit cards and they usually display a sign that will say in English "Card OK". Occasionally the card reader the drivers use will not work if you are in an area where the signal is weak, in which case you will have to pay in cash. Remember, you cannot use credit cards to pay for the limousine bus and rail services from the airport.

Pre-paid cards are becoming increasingly popular for use on trains, subways and buses. They can also be used to make small purchases in station kiosks, from vending machines and in some taxis. The cards have names like Suica and Pasmo and can be topped up at most stations.

Communications

According to Japan's Foreign Press Centre, the number of cellular phone users in the country had reached 96.7 million as of March 2007. The breaking up of NTT (until the mid 1980s a monopoly) opened up the market to fierce competition and the later introduction of mobile number portability fueled the flames. It is not unusual for providers to offer phones completely free of charge

---

[4] Foreigners are required to register with the Ward Office in the area in which they live within the first 90 days after arrival.

4

to those signing up for a wide menu of services designed to lure people away from their existing provider. Meanwhile the makers of cell phones vie with each other to bring out smaller, ever more sophisticated models that also serve as cameras, video cameras, television sets, music players, PDAs and so on. It is quite common to see entire rows of people on the subway sending and receiving text messages, listening to their favourite music downloads or even watching digital television programmes in high definition! The transport authorities stress the importance of keeping mobiles in silent, "manner", mode and to turn them off entirely when in the area of the priority seating which is designed for the elderly, those with disabilities and heart pacemakers, and pregnant women. Given that this is Japan, most people comply.

It would be unwise to assume that the mobile you use at home will work in Japan: check carefully with your provider. Fortunately, it is possible to rent mobiles relatively cheaply on arrival at the airport. Alternatively, if you are making your arrangements through a reliable travel agent, you can arrange to have a phone waiting for you when you check in to your hotel.

Internet use has also soared in Japan over the last five years or so, particularly broadband thanks in part to the fact that Japan's broadband fees are the lowest in the world .

Some of the international hotels in Japan's major cities offer teleconferencing facilities but they tend to be very expensive indeed.

Media

Broadcasting in Japan is in the hands of the publicly supported (non commercial) NHK and something in the order of 130 commercial stations. Cable and satellite are also widely available. By 2011, all of Japan's television programmes will be digital. Radio stations also abound, both FM and AM. NHK and some of the commercial stations offer bi-lingual (English and Japanese) news programming at certain times of day and feature films are frequently broadcast in bi-lingual format. Additionally,

[5] Source: International Telecommunications Union

with satellite and cable, it is possible to receive CNN, Fox and BBC World News, as well as the Discovery Channel, National Geographic and a variety of sports channels. Most of the international hotels in Japan's major cities will offer at least CNN and BBC World News and a selection of pay-per-view movies.

4

Japan has a number of locally produced English-language newspapers: the *Japan Times*, the *Yomuiri Shimbun*, the *Mainichi Shimbun*, and the *International Herald Tribune-Asahi*. Additionally, the Financial Times is also printed in Japan, meaning that the Tokyo edition appears before that in London as a consequence of the time difference (Japan is 9 hours ahead of GMT). Bookstalls in major hotels often carry other international newspapers but they are naturally a few days out of date by the time they arrive here.

Getting around

Japan's cities are blessed with clean, efficient, reliable and inexpensive public transportation systems. Buses, subways, and railways make getting around relatively painless, although in the major cities it may be best to avoid the morning and evening rush hours when overcrowding can be a serious problem. Major hotels can usually provide local maps in English and the colour-coded signage in most stations is very easy to follow. Many trains and subways in Tokyo now have pre-recorded English language announcements. All public transport in Japan has "priority seating" areas which are clearly marked, and are intended for the elderly, people with disabilities and heart pacemakers, pregnant women or women with babies or infants. Some city subway lines designate a "Women Only" carriage at certain times of day (usually the first or last carriage on the train).

Inter-city travel in Japan is also convenient and efficient (though it can in some cases be expensive). Japan has numerous regional airports and regular domestic flights criss-cross the country with sometimes surprising frequency. The rail network (including the various Shinkansen – "bullet train" – services) is extremely well developed. Additionally, luxurious limousine coaches

Trains

71

4

offer sometimes overnight travel along the nation's express highways.

Taxis in Japan either belong to the fleet of a major chain (such as KM, Odakyu, Keio etc) or they are privately owned: the so-called "kojin" (individual) taxis. The regulations governing what and how they charge are basically the same. These days, satellite navigation systems are finding their way into Japanese taxis, but you can't assume that every taxi you take will have one or that – even if they do – the driver will know how to use it.

Taxis are plentiful in the cities but very few drivers speak anything other than Japanese. It is a good idea to have a map (*in Japanese*) to your destination. If you are to visit a company or client ask them to send you such a map in advance. Your hotel may also be able to help you. Do not assume that your driver will know the way to your destination, even if it is very well-known; he may not even know where he is when he picks you up! With very few exceptions, street names in Japan's cities mean nothing and there is no Japanese equivalent of "the knowledge" that London's black cab drivers must acquire.

The passenger door of Japanese taxis is opened and closed by the driver; don't be tempted to do it yourself as it can interfere with the mechanics. The law dictates that you must wear a seatbelt when riding in a taxi; if you don't and the taxi is stopped both you and the driver will be held accountable. Fares are indicated on a meter and are calculated on the basis of a combination of distance and time. There are additional charges for late night journeys (also metred) and you will also be responsible for any highway[6] tolls incurred. There is no tipping; to the contrary, some taxi drivers will offer their passengers candy or gum in what is termed in Japanese "service". Please do not refuse this offering even if you do not intend to consume it. Smile and say thank you. You will make the driver's day.

Most of the major hotels can arrange for private limousine hire service if you feel you would like to be

---

[6] Even within the city certain roads – usually elevated expressways – are subject to tolls.

chauffeured around town. But, unless you are a celebrity who doesn't want to be spotted, public transport is a better (and much less expensive) choice, at least in the major cities. Roads can be severely congested, especially on what is known as *go-to-bi*: the 5th, 10th, 15th, 20th and 25th of the month. These are dates on which, traditionally, businesses settle their affairs (often in cash) and people are more than usually on the move.

It is also possible to rent a car. In order to do so you will need a valid international drivers license which you should organise before you leave for Japan. Traffic in Japan keeps to the left (as in Britain) and the rules of the road are in keeping with international standards. Parking is rigorously controlled: you cannot park on the street unless there are parking meters and there are not all that many of them available. Some public buildings and most department stores have parking lots, as do major hotels. There are a number of small temporary parking lots available, often on plots of land where buildings have been demolished and where new developments are planned. Japan has a policy of zero tolerance for driving under the influence of alcohol.

Over the last few years the Japanese government has made a serious effort to correct what was a major problem in Japan's cities, installing elevators and ramps to allow the disabled traveller easier, barrier-free access to subway stations, public buildings and so on. Though there is still room for improvement, such efforts are very welcome, as is the increasing trend toward banning smoking except in strictly confined smoking areas.

Shopping

In the major cities it is not uncommon to find areas dominated by large department stores such as Odakyu, Tokyu, Isetan, Mitsukoshi, Seibu and so on. Such stores are generally open daily from 10.00 to 18.00, closing one day a week (usually a Wednesday or Thursday). The basement floors are often the food area (well worth a visit even if you're not buying) and the top floors usually house a number of different kinds of restaurant (also worth visiting especially if you intend to eat there). Department stores in Japan are generally well laid out

4

and sell a tremendous range of goods. Service is first rate, polite and efficient and the way in which the sales staff wrap goods has to be seen to be believed. It is truly a work of art.

Tokyu Hands is a specialist chain of stores that sell an astonishing variety of goods from DIY and camping equipment to arts and crafts and hobby goods, from cosmetics to stationery and everything in between. You can spend hours browsing and there'll be no pressure from salespeople expecting you to buy.

At the other end of the scale are the Hyaku-en (One hundred Yen) shops which sell a great variety of items each at ¥100 or thereabouts. While not everything on sale is of the finest quality, there are often some genuine bargains to be had.

Cameras, computers and electronics goods are widely available at such chains as Bic Camera, Ishimaru Denki, Laox, Yamagiwa and so on. In Tokyo, the Akihabara district is known as "Electric City" because of its concentration of such shops. Most have a Duty Free area. Remember if you are buying electronic items that Japan's standard is 100 Volts, alternating at either 50 or 60 cycles, depending on which part of the country you are in. Plugs are generally twin flat bladed. The Duty Free shops will sell items with international specifications. You will need to present your passport to take advantage of Duty Free prices.

It is still possible, even in major cities, to find traditional shopping streets (*Shotengai*) where the shops have been in the same family for generations and where a visit is akin to stepping back in time.

Minding your manners

To make a sweeping generalisation, the Japanese are unfailingly polite (unless you happen to be in an overcrowded subway car at the height of the rush hour when almost anything goes; yet another of those pesky contradictions!) so it's as well to pay attention to a few of the basics when it comes to manners.

Japanese individuals who are used to dealing with foreigners will normally be quite happy to shake hands on meeting but generally physical contact is not encouraged. A bow is the more appropriate way of greeting and parting. There is an elaborate, hierarchical choreography depending on the relative status of those involved, but as a foreigner – especially a visiting one – you will not be expected to play a part in it or to know what degree the angle of your bow should be. A short, smart bending of the waist will suffice.

It is customary in Japan to refer to another person by their family name and to add the suffix *san* (meaning Mr/Mrs/Ms) as in Sato-san. (There is a more formal suffix *sama*, and the yet more formal *dono*, but you need not be concerned with these.) Some Japanese, especially those who have lived and worked abroad, adopt a western given name (Ken is very popular for some reason; perhaps because the Japanese first name Kentaro lends itself readily to such abbreviation). They may ask you to call them by this name. Even then, it would be polite to add the suffix and call them Ken-san. You do not use san when referring to yourself and, strictly speaking, san is not used when referring to a work colleague; the family name alone is used.

The Japanese love to offer hospitality and it is highly likely that you will be invited to a typical Japanese restaurant or bar. As a rule this will mean removing your shoes at the main entrance. Make sure your socks have no holes in them. You will be given a pair of slippers to wear on the wooden floors, but if you are then shown to a room or area with tatami mats on the floor, leave the slippers where the wooden floor ends. You do not walk on *tatami* in slippers. If in the course of the evening you need to take a comfort break you will find in the toilet another pair of slippers expressly for use in that small room. Try not to make the mistake (which most foreigners do at least once) of returning to your table wearing the toilet slippers. Doing so will provoke either much embarrassment or great hilarity, depending on how much sake has been drunk.

In some restaurants you will sit on cushions on the floor (it is not necessary to adopt the formal Japanese posture

Etiquette

4

4

of kneeling with your feet tucked under you; a guarantee of pins and needles). If you are lucky you will be seated in a *hori-kotatsu* – you still sit on the floor but there is a recess under the table for your legs so it is like sitting at table and thus more comfortable for most westerners.

It is not considered polite to pour your own drink; allow your host or someone else at the table to pour for you and then pour for them in return. If you decide you have had enough to drink, leave your glass full; each time you empty it, it will be refilled, especially if you are in an establishment where there is a hostess on hand.

Table manners are really a matter of common sense; watch how your Japanese hosts behave and follow suit. If in doubt, ask. It is OK to slurp noodles (some say it is the only way to enjoy them properly). You *can* – indeed, sometimes *should* – pick up your bowl. But don't be tempted to gesture with your chopsticks and don't on any account stick them upright in your rice bowl; that mimics something that occurs in Japanese funerals.

It is polite to return hospitality and, if your trip allows, you may want to invite your contacts for drinks or to dinner. If you do so, be careful not to "upstage" them; don't invite them to somewhere significantly more expensive than where they took you. Equally, don't go so far down market that it will be insulting.

You may wish to give gifts to your contacts, especially people who have been helpful. If so, please be sure that your gift is appropriate and well wrapped. Small items from your home country will always be welcome. But a word of caution: never give anything in units of four as one way of reading the Japanese character for the number four sounds like the Japanese word for death.

5

getting down to business

getting down
to business

This chapter provides elementary
guidance on the etiquette of business

Knowing your place (and theirs!)

Doing business in Japan is all about rituals. The better you understand them, the better impression you will make and the greater your chances of success. Above all else keep in mind the need for patience. Patience is more than a virtue in Japan; it is a quality that can make the difference between closing a contract and fleeing in frustration. Don't be in a rush, don't expect things to happen all at once and don't expect your interlocutors to do things your way. Remember that within a Japanese company (indeed any Japanese organisation) there is a distinct hierarchy and a set of rules that determines how just about everything is done.

The first two or perhaps three meetings you will have with your Japanese contacts will really be all about getting to know each other and setting out to build a relationship. Rarely will any actual business get done. But don't consider this a waste of time. Relationships in Japan are of tremendous importance and since the Japanese look for long-term commitment in business they will want to make sure that you are the right partner for them. Be prepared, therefore, to invest the same amount of time and effort as they do; in the long term it makes for a closer and more rewarding business relationship based on mutual trust.

The business basics

Let's suppose you're setting out for your first business meeting with a potential client or customer. You will, of course, be appropriately dressed and will have with you a good supply of *meishi* (name cards) hopefully carried in a case designed for that purpose, with a second compartment to hold the cards you collect from others. It is very important that you are not late; the Japanese put great store by punctuality. So make sure you allow plenty of time to get to your appointment. If possible, have the company send you a map to the meeting place ahead of time. Check with the staff at your hotel on the best way of getting to the venue. Depending on distance and time of day, public transport might be much quicker (and certainly less expensive) than taking a taxi.

5

If you are taking the subway, check on which station you need to get off at and which is the closest exit to the building you are going to. Subway stations in Tokyo can be very large and extend across whole city blocks. Taking the wrong exit can be very confusing and waste precious time.

If you do decide to take a taxi make sure you have a map in Japanese for the driver's convenience (and in case he has to ask at a police box for directions). Don't expect the driver to know where you want to get to, even if it appears to be a well-known building. It is not unknown for taxi drivers in Tokyo to claim they don't know where Tokyo Station is, for example.

Ask your hotel to advise on the time you need to reach your destination and add a little extra in case you get lost. Also ask if there are any well-known landmarks around the building you are visiting. Remember that with very few exceptions street names do not mean a great deal in Japanese cities. If the taxi has a satellite navigation system, it helps to have the exact address of the location and telephone number. Carry a card showing the location of your hotel in case you need to take a taxi back (you can't assume the driver will know even the best of them).

When you arrive at the company you are visiting, give the receptionist your name card and announce who you are visiting. You will be met and escorted to the room where the meeting will take place. The order of seating is very important and your escort will usually indicate where you should sit. If they don't, please ask.

It is highly unlikely that you will meet with only one other person, even if you are yourself alone, especially in the early stages. Typically, a number of company representatives will take part. This is largely due to the fact that no one will wish to take individual responsibility for what transpires in the meetings and also because no single person at the meeting will have the power to make any decisions. Their collective responses to what is discussed in the meeting will later be discussed further with the next level up in the company's management hierarchy where the decision will be made to go forward or not.

Management style in a typical Japanese company is from the bottom up with practically everyone being consulted through a process known in Japanese as *nemawashi* (roughly translated as consensus-seeking, it is actually an agricultural term to describe the practice of binding the shoots of something that you are about to plant to help ensure its growth; a nice thought when applied to a new business relationship).

When the company representatives enter the room, it is time to exchange meishi. *This is an extremely important* ritual and you should try very hard to get it right. When presenting your own name card, do so with both hands and make a small bow. As you do so, introduce yourself by saying, for example, "I am John Smith, General Sales Manager of Brown Ink Company. Thank you for seeing me today."

When you receive a card in exchange, again take it with both hands and spend a moment to study it carefully. This may feel awkward at first, but it is part of the ritual. Your Japanese contact will say something like, "Suzuki Insatsu, kokusai seirusu no, Watanabe-desu. Hajimemashite!" (I am Watanabe, from the International Sales Department of Suzuki Printing Company. Pleased to meet you.) You repeat this procedure with all of the meeting's participants. Then, when you sit down at the meeting table, place the name-cards in front of you in the order corresponding to where the person named sits on the opposite side of the table.

Treat the *meishi* with great respect. Don't use them to clean beneath your finger nails or pick your teeth and don't be tempted to write on them, at least not in the presence of the people who've given them. It is OK when back at the hotel to write on them the date of the meeting or a keyword that will help you remember something specific about a given individual but you should never do so at the time of the meeting. You should also treat your own name cards with respect. If you toss them around or allow them to become dirty and dog-eared, it sends the completely wrong message about you and – much more importantly – the company you represent.

5

5

The *meishi* ritual (which only happens the first time
you meet someone) is very important because it allows
everyone involved to understand exactly how each fits
into the hierarchy, who is senior to whom, who has
authority and who does not. Job titles in Japan do not
always correspond to a direct equivalent in Europe or
North America, but a rough guide is as follows:

Japanese	English
Sha-in	Staff member
Kakaricho	Supervisor
Kacho	Section Chief
Jicho	Deputy Department Head
Bucho	Department Head
Torishimariyaku	Director
Jomu Torishimariyaku	Managing Director
Semmu Torishimariyaku	Senior Managing Director
Fuku-Shacho	Vice President
Shacho	President
Fuku-Kaicho	Vice Chairman
Kaicho	Chairman

Once everyone is seated, you will be served with some
form of refreshment; green tea, coffee, iced-coffee in the
summer and sometimes these days mineral water. Don't
drink this until your host has invited you to do so. It is
even more polite to wait until he has taken a first sip.

The meeting will begin with small talk: how was your
flight, how do you like Japan (even if you've only been
there a single day)? Don't be in a hurry to make your
sales pitch. Remember that this is the period when the
people on the other side of the table will be sizing you
up, assessing your character, deciding whether they want
to go further down the path of developing a business
relationship. Maintain a friendly attitude and a good
posture: sloppy body language sends the wrong message.

Don't assume that the person who does the most talking
on the other side of the table is the most senior person
there – quite often the most senior manager will say
nothing – and don't be disconcerted if everyone on the
opposite side takes copious notes. These will be needed
for the various internal meetings that will inevitably
follow your visit.

Once you start discussing the business plan, stay focused on the key areas: where can you add value, why are you the right partner, why is the Japanese company your first choice? Don't offer more information than you are asked for; the Japanese tend in any case to be extremely demanding, but it is not necessary to divulge information you are not asked for. Answer the questions you are asked without adding anything more is a good rule of thumb.

If you are using an interpreter, avoid the temptation to speak to her and instead address the person on the other side of the table who is speaking to you. When a response is being interpreted for you, look at your interlocutor and nod from time to time to indicate that you understand what is being said. Don't be afraid to ask for clarification if you happen not to understand a point that is being made. A simple misunderstanding at this stage could have serious consequences later. You will use the polite suffix –san after people's family names. You will not of course use it of yourself (and strictly speaking, not of anyone else from your company who might be with you).

Don't be afraid of silence. The Japanese are comfortable with periods of silence in meetings whereas western business people tend to want to fill them. The result is often that the western party makes unnecessary concessions. Prepare yourself for this kind of situation: if there is a silence in the proceedings what will you choose to occupy your mind rather than feeling the need to leap in and say something?

If you are making a presentation, it is useful to have ready a version of it in Japanese that you can hand out. Even if those you are meeting can speak English this will help their understanding and it is a small courtesy that will be appreciated. (But make sure the Japanese is accurate and professionally presented).

Try to keep your visit to the time slot that was originally agreed, unless your interlocutors indicate they would like to extend it, in which case don't say you are unable to do so (a good reason – among many others – for not trying to pack too many meetings into a single day). When the people on the other side of the table start tidying up their papers or putting your name card in their meishi-holders,

5

you know the meeting is about to wind up. Tidy up your own papers and thank everyone for their time, perhaps adding that you look forward to a further meeting in the future.

If you are invited back for another meeting, don't be surprised to find some different people attending or to be asked some of the same questions you were asked before. Stay patient and answer them in a polite and friendly manner. This is all part of the need to build consensus within the Japanese company. The larger the company, the more departments are likely to be involved and they will all want to have their chance at quizzing you and having their say about a potential business relationship.

When the business discussions begin to get serious (and this may not happen until a later business trip) don't shift your position on the original sales pitch you have made. Don't be too ready to agree to conditions that make you uncomfortable or accept requests for major concessions on such things as pricing. If you do so it may be taken as a lack of confidence in your own products or services. Be polite in declining anything that is not acceptable but show willingness to be flexible where it seems expedient. It goes without saying that you should never promise anything unless you know you can deliver on it.

Don't jump to conclusions. When the Japanese say "yes" they more often that not mean "yes I have heard what you have said"; they are not necessarily agreeing to a request. On the other hand the Japanese are generally uncomfortable giving you an outright "no". Phrases such as "that might be a little difficult", "I'd like to give this more thought later" and so on are indicators that what you are offering is not necessarily enough to clinch a deal. However, within the bounds of courtesy be persistent; they may just be testing your commitment to your offer. Don't be too disappointed if no firm business comes out of your early meetings. You will have started along the path to building a relationship and one that you should see as being long term.

There are several case studies in the annals of international business history where a foreign company has concluded after several such meetings that their proposal has not

been accepted and has given up on their potential
Japanese partner only to have the Japanese side suddenly
come back and expect things to happen immediately.
Don't make the same mistake; it isn't over till it's over.

Business entertainment

In Japanese business, much goes on behind the scenes,
outside of the office over a few beers or perhaps an
informal meal. Department heads invite their staff out
occasionally so that they can get the kind of feedback
about what's going on in the office that would simply
not be discussed in the course of business hours. If the
office routine is locked into ritual formality, these
"social" meetings tend to be quite the opposite:
almost anything goes.

It is quite likely that at some stage you will be invited
out by your Japanese contacts, especially if they are
beginning to feel positive about the potential for the
business relationship. Take the opportunity to join in;
you are putting in place another piece in the jig-saw
puzzle that one day may become a partnership. Watch
your hosts carefully for hints on how to behave; whether
or not it's OK to take off your jacket at the table and so
on. Relax with them if you can but not to the extent that
you make careless comments that might reflect badly on
your business discussions. Drink in moderation, even if
your hosts don't. Actually, many Japanese find it hard
to deal with even small amounts of alcohol and quite
quickly get very red in the face. This does not always
mean that they are drunk, simply that they are unable
easily to metabolise the alcohol.

Chapter Four deals with matters of etiquette in bars
and restaurants.

It is not uncommon for foreign visitors to find
themselves taken to venues where karaoke is on
the menu. Some can be quite elegant and elaborate
establishments, others less so. The purpose of them is,
however, the same: to get you on your feet and singing
along to the "empty orchestra" backing. This is not
everyone's cup of tea but should you find yourself in this
situation, it pays to shut your eyes and think of whatever

5

business deal you are trying to close. Have at least one well known song that you can get through without entirely emptying the bar. To refuse entirely, even if you can't manage the whole song, could put a damper on the evening and who knows how that might affect future contacts?

Help on the ground

5

Hopefully you will have done a good deal of homework preparing for your visit to Japan. But the unexpected could occur and you may feel you need help or specialised information. Most of the international hotels (certainly those listed in this handbook) have business or executive centres that are very resourceful. They have multi-lingual staff that often have other business skills besides. They can arrange to have name-cards printed for you, fix up interpreters, make your travel arrangements, advise you on how to spend a spare half day and so on.

Your country's embassy or consulate is there to help, and a list of these is given in Appendix 1. There you will also find a list of the various Chambers of Commerce that have offices in Japan. From the Chambers you will be able to find the names and contact details of lawyers, tax advisers, shipping companies, and so on. The Chamber may also be able to introduce you to a member who is in a similar business or who has a similar profile. Speaking with someone who has already done what you are attempting to do can sometimes help you to avoid making the mistakes they might have done. Japan is a very large market, foreign companies have a small share and there is a sense in which many foreign firms are happy to help even potential competitors to increase that share.

The Japan External Trade Organisation

(www.jetro.go.jp/) has extensive resources and is a useful source of both information and practical support. The Tokyo Metropolitan Government's Business Entry Point (www.tokyo-business.jp/eng/entrypoint/index.html) is also a valuable resource and if you are visiting other major urban centres, local city governments often have bi-lingual websites that include contact details for any international departments or affiliated organisations that offer help to the foreign business traveller.

Here are 12 useful dos and don'ts for doing business in Japan'

1. Take things slowly. English comprehension may not be as good as it appears. Keep interventions simple and straightforward. The same is true if an interpreter is used. Make your interventions in short, easily translatable burst. Don't use sporting metaphors. If you must make jokes, keep them very simple.

2. Construct a short but warm introductory statement for each meeting. This should not be a sales pitch. It should explain why you're there, how long you'll be there, the sort of people you are seeing during your visit, and any particular previous contact you've had with Japan.

3. Then, after you and your interlocutor have made your respective introductory statements, make your sales pitch. But try to use the same sales pitch for all your meetings. In effect, decide what the five or six crucial points you want to get across during your entire visit are, and keep repeating them with all those you meet and in speeches you make.

4. Personal posture is important. Sit firmly in chairs at meetings even if they are armchairs. Don't slump, don't cross your legs and do maintain a fairly formal style. Don't blow your nose noisily. Don't drink tea offered to you before your host has indicated that you do so. Shake hands at the beginning and end of meetings. Never be late. Don't overrun the designated period for the meeting unless your interlocutor clearly wants to extend it. Don't hog the conversation.

5. Do not be worried if you feel you wish to read out a previously prepared note. Your interlocutor may well do this. Indeed, in making an impact, it's often more useful to read out a note and then leave it as an aide memoire.

6. Take business cards with you and have plenty available. They should be printed in Japanese on the reverse.

7. If you are taking gifts, make sure they are well wrapped, if possible professionally. Tatty

Source BCCJ website (www.bccjapan.com) used by permission.

wrapping paper is a British disease; as are cheap, tatty gifts. They indicate a discourtesy to the recipient. Do not give the gift until the end of the meeting. Don't be fazed if you have given a gift and not received one. You will have scored a point. Don't open the gift after receiving it; if it's not very good it will embarrass your host. If you open it, your host will also have to open yours and that could embarrass you.

8. Don't be afraid of silences. Sit tight and wait for something to happen. It's a common Western flaw in the Far East to feel that silences have to be filled. In negotiations, for instance, this normally means that the Westerner ends up conceding something.

9. Do pay self-evident respect to Japan's extensive history, unique culture and enormous economic achievements. No need to go over the top, but it does no harm to indulge in some well-placed flattery.

10. Enquire about your host's education, background, family, hobbies etc. Give information about your own. This is part of the sharing of contacts which helps build up a relationship.

11. For formal speeches, have a prepared text for distribution beforehand. The audience will follow this as you give it, dramatically improving comprehension. Impromptu or off-the-cuff changes risk being missed, or worse, mistranslated.

12. On taking the first drink at meals, toast your host by raising your glass to him and to those around you before you drink. Don't drink until it is time for those toasts to take place.

6

Japanese industries – a snapshot

Japanese industries – a snapshot

This is an overview of some
industrial sectors of the nation,
and where industries stand today

Industrial reform

Before taking a look at a few sectors of Japanese industry, it may be interesting to reflect for a moment on the current situation. Much has been written about Japan's extraordinary rise over the past half century as an industrial powerhouse and economic giant. But the post war years have seen a number of significant changes in Japan's industrial structure; some have been good, others less so. Once the country was back on its feet following the Occupation, the share of primary industries started to fall while secondary industries – for example heavy manufacturing and chemicals – enjoyed huge spurts of economic growth right through the 1960s, reaching over 43% of GDP by 1970; a peak. As their own golden age waned, helped in no small measure by the oil crises of the early 1970s, tertiary industries such as wholseale and retail, financial services and real estate experienced substantial growth reaching more than 72% of GDP in 2005[1].

At the time of writing there is renewed significant turbulence in world markets and it remains to be seen how Japan as one of the G20 will react in an effort to protect its economy and industry. Japan is short on natural resources and the current high level of the yen is good news in that regard; it can buy more. On the other hand, the country is also heavily dependent on exports and almost everything that it produces now is a good deal more expensive than it was a matter of six months ago. But perhaps that is too simple an equation in a time when much more complex remedies may be needed.

G20

All that can be said, without calling down the hubris, is that Japan has in the last decade dealt with a near melt-down in its own banking system and despite dire predications at the time that the country was finished once and for all, proved yet again that it had the resources and capability to withstand serious problems and recover from them. At the time the country was criticised from overseas by those who felt the government was taking too long to act. But the social

---

[1] Sources: various including the Cabinet Office and the Foreign Press Centre Japan.

consequences of a knee-jerk reaction or a less-than-well thought through response would undoubtedly have caused more pain than was already inevitable.

The Prime Minister at the time, Junichiro Koizumi, showed determination in this area when, under his leadership, the Council on Economic and Fiscal Policy set out a series of revitalisation measures. The 2002 directives were intended to inject new health into the economy by creating special zones in which deregulation would encourage new industries (and especially technology) from the private sector. As of March 2007 a little over 900 such business plans had been approved.

Then in 2003, the government established the Industrial Revitalisation Corporation of Japan with the purpose of turning around financially distressed companies without passing on the cost of doing so to the taxpayer. When the IRCJ ceased operations in 2007 is had assisted over 40 such businesses.

It is hard not to feel since Mr Koizumi stepped down (victorious after his pledge to set in motion the privatisation of the Japanese Post Office – then the largest banking system in the world) that there has not been so steady a hand on the tiller. There has certainly been less appetite for deregulation and even for engagement with the foreign business community, which is unfortunate. Whether you like it or not, the world's economy appears set on the track of increasing globalisation and Japan cannot afford to be left behind. Nor – it has to be said – can her major trading partners afford for her to be so.

Now to some sector specifics, some of which may surprise:

Agriculture & fisheries

Japan is widely seen as an industrial nation so it is easy to forget that agriculture has always been important to its culture. Despite limited amounts of arable land (something like 13% of the total) you will find farming the length and breadth of the country, even on the steep slopes of the numerous mountains. Rice is the principle crop, but mikan oranges, apples, Japanese pears, grapes, and a wide variety of vegetables are also grown, as is tea. There is also a certain amount of dairy farming. Ten per cent of national production comes from the northernmost main island of Hokkaido. However, as a percentage of GDP agriculture has seen year-on-year declines and the farming population is rapidly ageing. The value of agricultural produce in 2006 was ¥8.3 trillion (US$ 85.5 billion). The nation imports virtually all of its wheat and soybeans. Ironically, though Japan is more than self-sufficient in rice, the changing lifestyle of the younger Japanese means the country must increasingly depend on the foods it has to import.

6

Historically, fishing has played a major role in the lives of the Japanese people but here again, the industry has been in decline since the late 1980s. In part this is due to the changing tastes of younger generations of Japanese who eat less fish and more meats and western style dishes, and in part due to the declining stocks of fish around the Japanese archipelago. In 2007, the total catch was 5.6 million tons, down 0.7% from the previous year.

Controversially, Japan still engages in whaling. It claims it does so for scientific reasons and that it only takes from sustainable sources. Anti-whaling groups and some governments claim that Japan is engaging in commercial whaling under cover of claims to science. Whatever, it is true that whale meat does turn up in certain restaurants (they are usually restaurants that specialise) and from time to time in supermarkets. The arguments can become strongly emotional, with some Japanese insisting that whaling is an important part of the nation's history and culture and that it is unfair for other cultures to insist they give it up.

The automotive industry

Think of Japan's automobile industry and you're most likely to think of the Toyotas and Hondas and Nissans in terms of the products that bear their marques: vehicles that are today exported all over the world. Indeed, in

[2] Source: The Statistics Bureau
[3] *ibid.*

6

2008 Toyota surpassed GM as the world's largest auto maker. But cars are only a small part of what makes this sector so vital to Japan; as a whole it covers a truly large range of industries. Given that every car on the road is made up of literally tens of thousands of parts, that is not at all surprising. Think of all the metals (both common iron and steel and the noble metals used in purification processes etc), the resins, the glass, the pumps and cables and everything else. Whether directly or indirectly, over five million people (close to 8% of Japan's working population) are involved in auto industry-related work which in turn is responsible for 17% of the total value of Japan's manufacturing shipments and for roughly 37% of the value of the machinery industries' combined shipments[4].

It is true that in 2008 there have been further signs of a slowdown in new car purchases domestically, and a comparable sluggishness in overseas markets. That should be seen against a history of six consecutive years of increasing production. In 2007 Japan's car makers produced 11.6 million units[5] up 1.0% from the year before. Nevertheless, questions remain over the future and at the time of writing most companies in the country's auto-related sector are beginning to lay off part time workers and shutting down plants for blackout periods, in order to reduce inventories.

In recent years the sector has been looking very seriously at the impact is has on global warming and the environment. Under the Kyoto Protocol, Japan pledged to reduce its annual GHG emissions volume to 6% below the 1990 level by 2010 and the government set out a plan to meet that promise. It covered all sectors of business and industry and the automobile industry was quick to react. Vehicles that run on alternative energy sources, such as electricity, natural gas, and diesel-alternative LPG are becoming ever-more common. As of 2006 more than 400,000 alternative-energy vehicles, including several fueled by hydrogen, were on Japan's roads and the number is certain to grow. Some makers (such as Nissan)

---

[4] Source: Japan Automobile Manufacturers Association Inc.
[5] Source: *ibid.*

put great store by fuel-cell cars but success in promoting these will also have much to do with how the makers and their partners develop the infrastructure that can provide an appropriate and efficient fuel supply.

But it is not just the performance of the vehicles themselves. The Japan Automobile Makers Association has proposed an action plan that will encourage makers to introduce measures at their plants to reduce CO_2 emissions by 10% by 2010. Additionally, under Japan's 2005 End-of-Life Vehicle (ELV) Recycling Law automobile manufacturers and importers are held responsible for the recovery, recycling and appropriate disposal of specific components, achieving a recycle rate of 95% by vehicle weight. This is the first such law in the world.

Consumer electronics

Japan has long been at the forefront in this sector. The country's strong background in semiconductor technology and miniaturisation have helped electronics makers launch thousands of innovative products which an eager Japanese consumer base has quickly adopted and which often then find enthusiastic customers all over the world. A recent customer survey estimates that the domestic consumer electronics market will reach ¥11 trillion (US$ 113 billion) by 2010 and that does not include the market for cell phones, itself a sector worth trillions and which becomes more sophisticated with every model released. 90% of Japanese cell phones include a camera and many can also receive digital television broadcasts.

Recent developments see an increased coming together of communications and entertainment functions. One such development is the E PC, a computer that looks like a video machine and which serves as a control centre for all the electronics equipment in the home. For some time now, electronic devices have allowed Japanese remote control of such household tasks as running a bath or turning on or off lighting, heating and air-conditioning.

[6] Source Ministry of Internal Affairs and Communications of Japan.

There is growing demand for digital products with manufacturers looking more towards LCD technology. There has been an almost complete shift from analogue to digital photography with even the cheaper cameras offering greater convenience of storage and connectivity through either Bluetooth or Wi-Fi. Increasingly, too, automakers are building navigation systems into their vehicles and the latest tend to be LCD monitors that can also be used with DVD players.

"Freeters"

Not itself an industrial sector but a phenomenon that affects many – if not most – and perhaps worth a mention as it speaks to fundamental changes in what is happening across much of Japan's workplace and which will impact on the country's ageing society.

The term itself seems to be a contraction of the English language "freelance" and the German "arbeiter" (the loan word *arbutaito* has long been used in Japan to denote part-time work). It is applied to people (usually between the mid-teens to early 30s) who are not in regular employment. The significance of this is not particularly the impact on unemployment figures per se, but the fact that once embarked on this particular path, it is highly unlikely that an individual will develop the work and social skills to enter a Japanese (or any other) company at a later date. He will be doomed to spend his working life in low-paid (and often unregulated, sometimes risky) jobs that command little respect and even less hope. The consequence of this is that he will most likely not be contributing to a tax base that is already dwindling to the point where it cannot adequately support the increasing number of retiring baby boomers. In addition, when the freeter himself reaches the age of retirement, what will he have to live on with no state or company pension to fall back on?

In some case people fall into this pattern because they drop out of school early and genuinely have no interest in building a career; such people crop up in most developed societies. In Japan, especially, there is some reluctance by some individuals to be seen as just another "company man". But there are many more who are less-than willing victims of Japan's burst bubble of the 1990s when companies stopped hiring in the large numbers they had been used to (especially high-school graduates). To put that into perspective, the total number of job openings offered to new high school graduates in 1990 was 1,343,000. In 1995 it was 643,000. By 2000, the figure stood at just 272,000.[7]

It should be remembered that in Japan, the labour laws are such that once a person has been hired as a *shā-in* (company employee) it is extremely difficult indeed for a company to lay them off. Labour law, and the various labour unions, set out to protect the employee above all else. When the bubble finally burst, finding themselves burdened with expensive staff superfluous to their needs, companies began to regulate the employment process to avoid being again caught in this trap by using so-called "atypical workers" – contract employees and part-timers, for example – whose labour rights were less rigorously protected. In doing so, they appear to have created a not-insignificant dent in Japan's much-vaunted employment system. Whether it is ultimately fixable is currently the subject of hot debate.

Pachinko

It may seem odd to include gambling by pin-ball machine in this chapter until you understand the size of the business it generates. Though mostly controlled by Japanese residents of Korean descent, at least one UK company has seen the advantages of investing into it.

Pachinko Parlours are literally everywhere all over Japan; they are impossible to miss, taking up large areas of expensive real estate around most stations in virtually every town and city. They are noisy, smoky and packed from morning till night with enthusiasts (roughly 30 million regular players a year) who buy small metal balls to feed into a kind of pinball machine. The aim is to win back more balls than you put in, but whether it takes any kind of skill to do so is debatable. You then exchange these for items such as boxes of soap powder

---

[7] Source: Japan Institute of Labour

or packs of cigarettes (because the parlours are not allowed by law to pay out cash). These you take around the corner to an un-named hole in the wall to cash them in. You get the cash, the hole in the wall gets a cut and the goods are returned to the parlour for recycling. Sounds flippant? Then consider this:

Astonishingly, *pachinko* employs more than three times the number of people who work in Japan's steel industry. It accounts for fully 40% of the country's leisure sector – including restaurants and bars – and its turnover, at something like ¥30 trillion (US$ 309 billion) is larger than that of the country's automotive industry. Further, if recent figures are to be believed, *pachinko* does not appear to be significantly affected by periods of economic uncertainty.

Pharmaceuticals

Japan's pharmaceutical industry is the second largest in the world, following the USA and it accounts for more than 80% of the country's total life-science market. It is a rather mature market yet – given the nation's rapidly ageing population – it is expected to show steady but slow growth. In 2007, sales of anti-body based drugs totaled ¥85 billion (US$874 million), four times the total in 2003[8]. While there are well over a thousand pharmaceutical companies in Japan, the top 20 account for almost 65% of overall sales[9]. While this sector has been traditionally difficult for foreign firms to break into, Japanese firms have made efforts to break into other markets through licensing and other arrangements. Trade organisations such as the American Chamber of Commerce in Japan and the European Business Council regularly lobby strongly for the opening up of the market and for the easing of a number of regulations that mean a lengthy and expensive testing regime for drugs that have been successfully tested and approved by authorities in the USA and Europe.

[8] Source: Biospectrum Asia
[9] Source: *ibid.*

Science & technology

Private sector investment has traditionally been the main driver of Japan's science and technology efforts. After a two year dip in the early 1990s, corporate R&D rebounded and reached a staggering total of ¥17.8 trillion (US$176 billion) in fiscal 2005[10].

Ever since 1995 there have been legally backed government efforts to stimulate original basic research in new areas and in 2001, as part of the Koizumi reforms the Council for Science and Technology Policy was set up as part of the Cabinet Office. The current plan (covering the period 2006-2011) allocates an R&D budget of ¥25 trillion (US$257.5 billion) and specifies four priority areas: life sciences, information technology, environmental sciences, and nanotechnology and materials. Additionally, there are four second-tier areas: energy, technological craftsmanship, infrastructure, and frontier (defied as outer space and ocean)[11].

The Japan Aerospace Exploration Agency (JAXA) was set up in 2002, bringing together the three agencies that had until then overseen Japan's space development programmes. As of February 2007 Japan had launched a total of 12 information gathering satellites, all but two of which have proved successful. The focus now is to encourage a satellite launching business with Mitsubishi Heavy Industries, strongly supported by the government, playing a principal role. Japan's technical capabilities do not appear to be in any doubt, but realistically it will have to find ways to make launches economically competitive if this idea is to go forward.

Another area of R&D which is attracting a good deal of attention is the efforts by such companies as Sony, Honda, and Toyota (among others) to develop robots. Osaka Prefecture and the City of Osaka also have some interesting initiatives[12]. Industrial robotics are, of course, nothing new with much of Japan's manufacturing plant using more robotic- than man- power. However, the new areas of R&D probe the development of more humanoid

JAXA

[10] Source: Ministry of Finance of Japan
[11] Source: Ministry of Education, Culture, Sports, Science and Technology of Japan
[12] See: http://www.osaka-saisei.jp/eng/business/

6

6

robots. Already prototypes have been built that are designed to assist people who are paralysed to walk, and there are various plans for "helper robots" that are designed to meet the expected need for more care for the elderly and infirm at the very time when the national birth rate is falling and there are fewer real humans to step up to the tasks. There are even robots that can help teach doctors to be better at their jobs. The more advanced androids can already serve tea – the Japanese green variety of course – talk, walk (including climbing and descending stairs) and some makers claim to be well on the way to creating robots that can actually think and, even, "intuit". Last but not least, for those who don't fancy dog hairs on the carpet or cat scratches on the paintwork, there are robot pets; cuddly, they're not: down, Rover!

Shipbuilding

In recent years Japan has held second or third place (South Korea is in the top spot) in terms of annual tonnage of ships built. From around 2005 global demand for new ships was boosted by an increased need for tankers and bulk carriers, supported by what was then a healthy US economy and a greatly increased desire by China to ship more crude oil and iron ore. It remains to be seen how the recent changes in the global economy will affect both shipping and shipbuilding, but the Japanese government is committed to keeping what it sees as a key industry "competitive in the world market while keeping its production base in Japan"[13].

One specific area in which Japan has the lead is in the state-of-the-art technology known as "Mega-Float"[14] designed to promote efficient use of ocean space. Highly 'quake resistant, this has tremendous potential for structures such as airports (it's claimed as large as 4,000-metre class is feasible), information back up centres, container terminals and even leisure facilities.

---

[13] Source: Ministry of Land, Infrastructure and Transport of Japan
[14] See: http://www.srcj.or.jp/html/megafloat_en/index.html
[15] Source: The Japan Iron and Steel Federation

Steel

Figures released by Japan's Ministry of Economy, Trade and Industry put iron and steel at the top of the country's production indexes for manufacturing industry in 2006. With the rise of China, Japan's main steel makers (Nippon Steel Corporation, JFE Holdings Inc, Sumitomo Metals Industries Inc, and Kobe Steel) have recently seen their consolidated incomes soar well beyond anything they experienced during Japan's own bubble economy . This rapidly increasing demand from China coincided with a significant re-alignment of the capitalisation of some of the world's major motor manufacturers: Nissan with Renault (still intact) and Daimler-Chrysler with Mitsubishi (now no more). The effect of these alliances was to put huge pressure on steel prices which the steel companies met by themselves consolidating (for example, in 2002, NKK Corporation and Kawasaki Steel Corporation established JFE Holdings). Declining sales of automobiles at home and aboard are bound to have an impact on the blast furnaces but it is difficult to predict how soon that will be felt.

China is more than self-sufficient in the kind of steel it needs for basic construction projects but still needs to import high-quality product for automotive production and electric sheet steel. Here again, demand is expected to decline in the short to medium term; the hope is that it will recover if the Chinese economy continues to remain strong and weather the recent turbulence.

Wine

Thanks to its climate (high humidty and periodic heavy rainfall) Japan is not ideally suited to viticulture, but wine made from grapes has been produced there for hundreds of years. The first commercial winery was established in 1875 in Yamanashi Prefecture which still today – along with areas of Hokkaido – is the centre of the country's wine production. Only companies that are licensed by the Ministry of Finance are permitted to

6

---

[15] Source: The Japan Iron and Steel Federation

make wine and today they number just over 200. Chief among them are Sapporo, Suntory and Mercian.

Though grapes are grown in quantity in Japan, only a very small percentage is used in wine-making. Wineries import grape concentrate and also blend what they produce with wine imported in bulk. Probably the most successful of the domestically produced wines are the sweet whites.

Wine consumption in Japan has increased dramatically over the last twenty years or so, in part due to the growth of the restaurant sector, but also due to the efforts of foreign makers from all over the world who now enjoy strong exports. South American, South African, Australian and Californian wineries compete successfully with the more traditional French, German and Italian labels.

7

setting up a
business in Japan

setting up a business in Japan

The aim of this section is to
provide a sweeping overview
for the visitor who is considering
the possibility of a local office.

Let's say you've had a successful visit to Japan, done your homework and have decided to set up an operation there. How should you proceed?

The right answer is cautiously. It's not that's it's difficult to do; rather that there is more than one way to do it and deciding early on which is the right way for you could save you a good deal of frustration, not to mention money. There are any number of consulting firms that can help you make that choice according to your particular circumstances. The purpose of this chapter is to give a very simple general overview of the options that might help you in your discussions. It is not intended to be a complete guide and it is very important that you take the appropriate professional advice.

7

What are my choices?
There are basically four types of operations:
* Representative Office
* Branch Office
* Subsidiary Company
* Limited Liability Partnership

Which one will work for you depends on a number of factors, including what it is you want to do, how much money you have to play with, what kind of business you are in, and where you want to go with it.

Representative office
This is the simplest kind of operation and it does not require any capitalization or formal registration of any kind. It's often the way a new-to-market company chooses to begin, using the office to gather information, promote products and services, test the market for potential employees and generally make preparations to advance to one of the stages below. However, a representative office cannot engage in sales activity and will not normally be able to open bank accounts or enter into contracts such as leases. Usually, the head office will be the signatory to any such agreement. Alternatively (assuming the Japanese partner agrees) the person running the office may sign in an individual capacity.

Branch office

A branch office has no independent legal status and is generally not expected to act independently of the head office. However, once established, it is possible to open bank accounts and enter into agreements such as leases in the branch's name. A branch must be registered with the Legal Affairs Bureau and that can only happen when a representative is appointed and an office space is secured. There is no requirement for capitalization.

Subsidiary company

This is an entity that is independent of the parent company and recognised under Japan's Corporate Law. There is a choice between a joint stock corporation (Kabushiki-Kaisha, designated as KK) and a limited liability company (Godo-Kaisha, designated as LLC). The company must be capitalized (in theory it is possible to do so for ¥1) and registered with the Legal Affairs Bureau.

Limited Liability Partnership

It is also possible to set up operations using a Yugen Sekinin Jigyo Kumiai (LLP). Strictly speaking this is not a corporation. The rules of operation may be freely decided among the equity partners who each bear responsibility for taxes.

What are the tax implications?
Corporate taxes

A company having a main office in Japan is considered to be resident for tax purposes, even if there is no local management. It will be taxed on its worldwide income. A foreign corporation, on the other hand, will normally only be taxed on Japan-sourced income. The amount that is taxable is the excess of gross taxable revenue after deducting legitimate business expenses. The national standard rate of corporation tax is 30% where the company's share capital exceeds ¥100 million. A special rate applies to SMEs whose share capital is not more than ¥100 million, and that is 22% for the first ¥8 million of taxable income.

Additionally, there is a local inhabitant's tax which varies according the location and size of the company. This is calculated as a percentage of the national corporation tax. Prefectures also level a Local Enterprise Tax of roughly 41% (42% in Tokyo). Dividends, interest on loans and royalties paid to nonresidents are subject to withholding tax of 20% (15% on deposits and bonds). Employers must withhold income tax and social security at source, and must also contribute to social security; the employer portion is a little over 13.5%. Various forms of stamp duty are imposed on the execution of taxable documents.

A variety of rules and regulations apply to such issues as transfer pricing and tax havens etc that are beyond the scope of this book and should be addressed by the appropriate professional advisors.

Personal taxes

A foreign businessman who has lived in Japan for one year or more but five years or less in the preceding 10 years is considered a non-permanent resident for the purposes of taxation. Taxes are levied on Japan-sourced income and on income remitted to Japan. Permanent residents (for the purpose of taxation) are taxed on worldwide income, including both employment and investment income. The rate of taxation is progressive, with a maximum of 50%. Income tax is made up of two components; a national tax and that levied by the ward in which the taxpayer lives. Both are normally withheld at source, as are the social security payments. Stamp duty is charged on the execution of taxable documents.

Subject to some restrictions, deductions are allowed for such things as Japanese social insurance premiums, life- and earthquake-insurance, qualified medical expenses and certain charitable contributions. In addition there are allowances for the individual, a dependent spouse and children under the age of 23. Individuals must file an annual tax return with the tax office responsible for the area in which they reside.

Value Added Tax

Called the consumption tax in Japan, it is levied on the supply of goods and services as well as the sales of lease

VAT

107

of assets. It is currently at 5% but the government has spoken to the need to raise this rate in the near future to help offset the dwindling tax base as the population ages and the number of those in employment falls.

Visas and immigration

If you intend to work in Japan you must obtain the appropriate working visa before arriving there (See the box for the various types of visa). It is not possible to secure a working visa while you are in the country. Applications for working visas must be made at Japanese Consulates or Embassies and, depending on the type of visa, a variety of documents will be required. The process can be quite time-consuming but it can be accelerated somewhat by obtaining a Certificate of Eligibility. This is issued prior to making a visa application by a regional immigration authority under the jurisdiction of the Ministry of Justice. It is evidence that the applicant fulfills various conditions of the Immigration Control Act, including those certifying that the activity in which the individual wishes to engage in Japan is valid and comes under a status of residence (excluding Temporary Visitor Status).

If the company you are going to work for is already established it is a simple matter for the HR department to apply for the Certificate and forward it to you. If you are setting up a company from scratch you can use a business consultant or an immigration lawyer. Another option is to use what is called an Adminisrative Document Lawyer, such as:

Mr Toshiyasu Maekawa
Administrative Document Lawyer
MAEKAWA OFFICE
3rd Floor TSK Bldg.
1-4 Kanda Suda-cho, Chiyoda-ku, Tokyo, 101-0041
Japan
Tel: 81-3-5207-6315 Fax: 81-3-5207-6375
E-mail: toshiyasu.maekawa@nifty.com

Mr Maekawa is certainly not the only practitioner in town but he enjoys a good reputation among both European and North American chambers of commerce.

The most common visas granted to foreign businesspeople are for the investor/business manager and the inter-company transferee. Each may be given for a one- or three-year period and may usually be extended by a similar term on application. (For details of the more specialized visas and what activities they permit see the homepage of the Ministry of Foreign Affairs of Japan at www.mofa.go.jp/)

Investor/business manager

This permits the holder to carry out activities to commence the operation of international trade or other business, to invest in international trade or other business and to operate or manage that business, or to operate or manage international trade or other business on behalf of foreign nationals (including foreign corporations) who have begun such an operation or have invested in such a business. The business in question must meet certain conditions of scale. Applicants who wish to engage in business management must fulfill certain conditions concerning work status and personal history.

Inter-company transferee

This permits the holder to carry out activities on the part of personnel who are transferred to business offices in Japan for a limited period of time from business offices that are established in foreign countries by public or private organizations with head offices, branch offices, or other business offices in Japan. Applicants must fulfill certain conditions concerning personal history and work status.

Setting up an office

Office rents in Tokyo are not what they were at the height of the so-called bubble but they are nevertheless still expensive when compared to many other cities both domestically and overseas. The quality of office space available has improved considerably in recent years as developers all over the capital have put up new buildings and significantly renovated others. Projects such as Roppongi Hills, Midtown, Shiodome, and in Marunouchi have expanded capacity and as the larger,

7

wealthier, companies have moved into these prestigious buildings, they have left behind more affordable and still very serviceable space. But it pays to shop around and seek the advice of the larger real estate agents. Your national chamber of commerce in Japan should be able to make the appropriate introductions (for a list see Appendix 1).

It is still possible to find relatively cheap space in certain areas of the city, usually in the so-called "pencil" buildings (because they are thin; usually one single space per floor). But be careful that such buildings conform to the latest earthquake resistance regulations. Many buildings put up much before 1984 are unlikely to do so, unless they have been retrofitted.

JETRO

For a completely new start-up it is possible to secure free office space in one of the Business Support Centres set up by the Japan External Trade Organisation (www.jetro.go.jp/). There is a limit to the amount of time you can spend there but it is often enough to allow you to explore the possibilities of a more permanent space. There is also the advantage of having on hand JETRO's advisors, a library and meeting rooms as well as other facilities. The Centres are not limited to Tokyo. Others are in Osaka, Nagoya, Kobe and Yokohama and you can find out more about them from any one of JETRO's numerous overseas offices or through the website.

There are a number of companies that offer fully serviced offices, among them Regus (www.regus.com) and Servcorp (www.servcorp.net/) and these can be a very convenient way of starting out, especially as they offer logistical support, answering the telephone in the company name, providing back-office type services and offering a variety of virtual office options. However, in the longer term they may prove more expensive than going it alone.

The British Industry Centre, located in the Yokohama Business Park (a convenient 30 minute train ride from central Tokyo) offers extremely high quality office spaces of various sizes and at heavily subsidised rents. The City of Yokohama also offers a number of financial and other incentives to companies electing to be based there.

Originally an initiative of the British Government together with the British Chamber of Commerce in Japan, the City of Yokohama and Nomura Real Estate, it offers significant advantages over and above the various financial ones. There is a standardised lease, for example, negotiated by professionals and fully checked by Japanese lawyers, and the BCCJ can make introductions to vendors and suppliers who all offer significant discounts on goods and services provided to BIC tenants. The Business Park itself has shops, restaurants, conference facilities, dental and medical clinics, a bank and a post office, and is within easy reach of Shin-Yokohama station (servicing the Shinkansen "bullet train") as well as Narita and Haneda Airports and the major Tomei Expressway between Tokyo and the Kansai region. Yokohama also offers residential properties that are generally less expensive than those in central Tokyo and has other amenities that appeal to the foreign business family (see Chapter Nine). For further details about the BIC and to arrange a visit contact the British Chamber at info@bccjapan.com.

Leases

The standard term for an office lease in Japan is two years and the right of renewal is all but universal. Tenants may be permitted to cancel the contract on six months notice or perhaps with a penalty of six months rent. On the other hand, the landlord has little power to terminate; the courts have historically sided with the tenant where disputes have arisen which is one reason why deposits are high and the screening process is lengthy. Landlords normally expect a prospective tenant to provide a guarantor before signing the lease.

Deposits

Expect to pay at least 12 months deposit (in some cases it might be as high as 24 months). Deposits are not interest-bearing and, although returnable, you can expect the landlord to keep a certain percentage of what you put down to pay for "making good" – putting the premises back to the condition they were in when you rented. Make sure you have a clear written understanding with the landlord when it comes to what you can do with the space you are renting; most will not

7

look kindly on major structural changes and many will insist that you use a vendor of their choice when it comes to making even minor ones.

Expatriate housing

The quality of housing in Japan – and especially Tokyo – has improved tremendously in recent years. However, if you are on a limited budget, it may prove difficult to find somewhere with all mod cons such as dishwashers and even fully fitted kitchens. Only the more recently constructed buildings will have such things as double (still less triple) glazing and the older apartment buildings tend to offer smaller spaces than many western families are used to.

Depending on location, size, associated amenities and a variety of other factors, you can expect to pay anything from ¥500,000 to ¥3 million per month for the kind of apartment that is considered suitable for western families. Occasionally in Tokyo (more often in Yokohama) stand-alone houses are available for rent at similar prices.

Many large foreign corporations have standing agreements with real estate companies so that their employees have no difficulty finding a place to live. If the employer contracts directly with the landlord, there can also be huge advantages (including in certain circumstances a tax advantage to both employer and employee). This is clearly a relatively painless way of finding a home, though it does restrict your individual choice to a degree.

If you are faced with finding something by yourself it pays to work with one of the experienced real estate agencies that are used to dealing with expatriates (see below). You are unlikely to have much success with approaches to individual landlords, especially if you are not fluent in Japanese. Even then, it is safer to work with an agent. Be as specific as you can when briefing the agent as to your preferred location(s) (bearing in mind access to international schools if relevant) budget, and any special requirements such as barrier-free access. Be careful if you use more than one agent not to let more than one of them show you the same apartment or house;

you may well end up paying an agency fee to all of them who do if you should choose to take it. Be sure to ask about all charges over and above the stated monthly rent. There is usually a caretaker's fee and in the more sophisticated developments a separate concierge fee. Parking is almost always additional and it can be extremely expensive indeed in central Tokyo. You will not be able to buy (or lease) a car in Japan unless you can prove you have off-road parking within a certain (small) radius of your home. Utilities – water, electricity and gas are all metred and billed monthly.

In addition to the agent's fees (usually one month's rent) you will be required to put down at least two month's deposit (often more for houses). As with office deposits, this is refundable but the landlord will normally keep some of it for "professional cleaning". There is, additionally, something called "key money" which is in effect a gift to the landlord of two to five month's rent which you will never see again. Some agents offer properties with "no key money" but finding somewhere of first rate quality without paying this fee is unlikely.

7

Leases, as for offices, are normally signed for two years with an option of renewing but it is not uncommon for a tenant to face a new set of agent's fees, a rise in the monthly rent and – in some case – some more "key money" at renewal.

Before signing the lease, the landlord will expect you to have provided a reliable guarantor who must normally be a Japanese national or at least a foreigner who has Permanent Resident status (roughly equivalent to the US Green Card).

Residential real estate agents
(Not an exhaustive list)
Ken Corporation Ltd
www.kencorp.com/

Mori Building KK
www.moriliving.com/

Plaza Homes
www.realestate-tokyo.com/

Overseas Corporation
www.overseas.co.jp/

Sun Realty
www.sunrealty.co.jp/

Serviced apartments

Another option, especially for the single businessperson, or for those on relatively short-term assignments is to rent one of the many serviced apartments offered by companies such as Oakwood Residences (www.oakwood.com/)

International schools

Families relocating to Japan are naturally concerned about the education of their children. Fortunately there are a number of good international schools around the country offering a variety of curricula. For example, Yokohama, Nagoya, Kyoto, Osaka, Kobe, Hiroshima, Fukuoka, Okinawa, Sapporo, and Sendai all have international academies.

In Tokyo, not surprisingly, there is a large choice, some of which are listed below. This is not exhaustive. Your own embassy or consulate in Japan should be able to provide you with more appropriate contacts (see the list in Appendix 1).

The American School in Japan
(http://community.asij.ac.jp/NetCommunity/Page.aspx?pid=200&srcid=-2)

The British School in Tokyo
(www.bst.ac.jp/)

International School of the Sacred Heart
(www.issh.ac.jp/)

Nishimachi International School
(www.nishimachi.ac.jp/)

Categories of Visa and Status of Residence

Visa	Status of Residence
Diplomatic Visa	Diplomat
Official Visa	Official
Working Visa	Professor
	Artist
	Religious Activities
	Journalist
	Investor/Business Manager
	Legal/Accounting Services
	Medical Services
	Researcher
	Instructor
	Engineer
	Specialist in Humanities/ International Services
	Intra-company Transferee
	Entertainer
	Skilled Labor
Temporary Visitor's Visa	Temporary Visitor*
Transit Visa	Temporary Visitor*
General Visa	Cultural Activities*
	College Student*
	Pre-college Student*
	Trainee*
	Dependent*
Specified Visa	Designated Activities+
	Spouse or Child of Japanese National
	Spouse or Child of Permanent Resident
	Long-Term Resident

(Source Ministry of Foreign Affairs of Japan)

7

* Statuses of residence not permitting work.
+ Whether work is permitted or not depends on the content of individual permits.

Tokyo

Detailed street maps are available in all major hotels

8

Tokyo

8

Tokyo

An introduction to Japan's
capital city, including where to
stay and what to eat

An introduction

Japan's capital city should rightly be referred to as The Tokyo Metropolis (Tokyo-to). One of Japan's 47 Prefectures, it is actually made up of 23 special wards, 26 cities, 5 towns and 8 villages, including those on numerous outlying islands, some as far as 1850 kilometres from central Tokyo itself. As of October 2007 the overall population was put at 12,790,000, more than 8.5 million of whom live in the 23 special wards. These once comprised the City of Tokyo but after the city was merged with Tokyo Prefecture in 1943, they became separate self-governing entities each with a mayor and a council. The Tokyo Metropolis itself is administered – as are the other Prefectures – by an elected Governor (currently the controversial nationalistic Shintaro Ishihara) and there is a special administrative arrangement in place between the metropolitan government and the special wards to ensure that this most densely populated area in Japan is uniformly served when it comes to utilities and other public services.

Tokyo was originally known as Edo (meaning "mouth of the estuary") and was renamed when it became the imperial capital in 1868: the literal meaning is Eastern (to) Capital (kyo). Long before that however, beginning in 1590 under the shogun Tokugawa Ieyasu, Edo grew into one of the largest cities in the world, a ranking it maintains today. The city benefited enormously from the western influences that were encouraged by the Emperor Meiji (1868-1912) following the opening up of the country. Brick buildings and paved roads began to appear, telecommunications were set up (initially between Tokyo and Yokohama) and British railway engineers helped build the first steam locomotive link between Shimbashi and Yokohama. Meiji era Tokyoites began to favour western fashions: bowler hats and bustles were the order of the day for those aiming at sophistication. The beginnings of a consumer society began to emerge; there were significant educational advances and a healthy respect for the performing arts began to develop. But the 20th century was to deal Tokyo two significant blows that set the city back considerably.

8

8

Strike one

On September 1st, 1923 at 11.58 a.m. the Kanto Plain was struck by an earthquake estimated at Richter 8 or above. The city and much of the surrounding area, including the Port of Yokohama, was devastated. A number of accounts suggest the shaking went on for several minutes and since the 'quake hit when many people were preparing lunch, fires broke out all across the city. These were fanned by strong winds from an approaching typhoon. All told more than 100,000 people died (some estimates put the toll as high as 142,000), the majority of these as a result of the fires, which burned for two full days. The destruction was so severe that many in government wanted to relocate the capital but the Home Minister at the time, Count Shinpei Goto, drew up a reconstruction plan for Tokyo that included creating parks all over the city that could be used as places of refuge in case of future disasters. Tokyo still has numerous designated evacuation areas and every year on September 1st, various drills are held in schools and other institutions throughout the city to remind residents of the importance of being prepared for when the next "Big One" strikes.

Strike two

Despite limitations on the amount of financing available, reconstruction following the 'quake continued into the beginning of the Showa Era (1926-1989) with the opening of Japan's first subway line between Ueno and Asakusa in 1927 and the completion of the Tokyo Airport at Haneda in 1931. But just ten years later came the second blow: the Pacific War. Specifically, towards the war's end the capital city was the focus of intense and relentless bombing raids, the heaviest of which occurred in March 1945 resulting in the loss of up to 200,000 lives and massive material damage. Essentially, though the atomic bombings of Hiroshima and Nagasaki were arguably more dramatic in nature, the carpet bombing of Tokyo was equally destructive, flattening the city and leaving its remaining 3.5 million people defeated and in despair.

Rebuilding

Just 17 years later the population had tripled to over 10 million. Japan's efforts to rebuild after its defeat in war were aided in no small measure by the outbreak of the Korean War in 1950; the US needed bases for its forces and to make special procurements. Japan was in the right place at the right time. By 1956 it had joined the United Nations and had embarked on a concerted drive to use emerging technologies to give it a competitive edge in the mass production (and marketing) of household appliances both for domestic but – arguably the more important – export consumption. Tokyo was, of course, at the centre of all of this and when it was selected to be the first Asian host of the Olympic Games in 1964, winning out in round one of voting over Detroit, Michigan, Vienna and Brussels, the city was given an enormous boost. The XVIII Olympiad became the first televised event to be broadcast across the Pacific. There were rebroadcasts all over the world, putting post-war Japan back on the map, the broadcasts signaled by Yuji Koseki's distinctive theme music.

The city's infrastructure benefited hugely – elevated expressways, new hotels and specially created venues that are still evident today. What is now the National Stadium hosted the opening and closing ceremonies as well as track and field and the Nippon Budokan – now one of the city's most popular concert venues and the place where the Beatles made their celebrated Japan debut – was built to accommodate the newly introduced judo events. Perhaps most striking was Kenzo Tange's Yoyogi Gymnasium complex which still today looks futuristic. Tokyo also drew attention as the starting point for the Tokaido Shinkansen, quickly dubbed the "bullet train". Running at 210 km/h in 1964 it was a transport breakthrough. Today's trains average 300 km/h and tests on conventional trains have been carried out up to 443 km/h. The proposed maglev trains anticipate speeds of over 580 km/h. Meanwhile, according to JR the average delay per train in 2008 was 0.4 minutes; this in a country prone to earthquakes, typhoons and other phenomena which are likely to disrupt transportation.

8

Prosperity

The 1970s saw the start of Japan's rapid and strong economic growth, despite the setbacks of the 1973 "oil shock". It was a decade, too, when Tokyo sought to change its image as one of the world's most polluted cities; pictures of traffic policemen taking "oxygen breaks" at the Ginza crossroads were not uncommon in the tabloids of the day. Serious measures were put in place to clean up the city's air and its rivers and as early as March 1971, the Tokyo Metropolitan Government introduced its "Programme to Protect Residents of Tokyo from Environmental Pollution" which quickly had the effect of reducing the amount of sulphur dioxide released by factories in and around the city.

This was the decade in which Japan began its impressive investment salvo into overseas markets, principally the USA and Europe (especially the United Kingdom). The country began to grow in confidence and with it, Tokyo sought to become more international. Going into the early 80s, foreign banks and law firms began setting up in the city, despite the seriously high prices of doing so and several restrictive regulations. Massive building developments began all over the metropolis and newly developed seismic technologies made it possible to build ever higher – a boon in space-hungry Tokyo.

The city was clearly hit by the bursting of the ensuing bubble (though not as hard as it might have been and not as lastingly as Osaka). But despite the faltering economy and the impact of the Asian financial crisis, Tokyo continued to build, with impressive new developments along the waterfront at Shiodome, Odaiba – built on what had once been the capital's garbage tip – and the complete regeneration of the old warehouse and factory area behind Shinagawa station. The city also saw huge new developments in the Roppongi Hills and Tokyo Midtown projects and the Marunouchi area in front of Tokyo station has also benefited from massive investment with buildings being renovated and new ones rising almost as if overnight.

8

An international city?

For all that, there is something of a puzzle about Tokyo that even those who know it well and love it find hard to fathom. It aspires to be a major centre of international finance to compete with London and New York, yet is banking system is so inefficient as to appear almost feudal, and the difficulties foreign firms can face in meeting regulatory requirements are a true disincentive in some areas (the legal profession, for example). Japanese companies are generally averse to being acquired by foreign ones, although there have been exceptions, and in one recent (2008) case the government actually intervened to prevent a foreign fund increasing its shareholding in a local entity. The extremely poor level of English (especially as compared to Seoul and Shanghai, for example) also works against Tokyo's stated interest in being truly international.

The country appeared to be making headway in resolving some of this during the tenure of Junichiro Koizumi (2001 – 06) who appeared to be a true champion of reform; witness his determination (and success) to privatize the Post Office (the world's largest bank). But in more recent years, despite claims to the contrary, there are some who feel that Tokyo has actually taken some backward steps.

None of which, however, should be taken as an argument to dismiss Japan because the business opportunities here are enormous. Getting in and getting it right may take a little time but the rewards are well worth it, as a properly planned visit will clearly demonstrate.

Hotels

Tokyo has some of the finest hotels in the world. To list them all would require a much larger handbook than this, so what follows is a sample of venues that have been tested to the satisfaction of the author and a number of discerning business associates. The omission of other hotels should not be taken to imply criticism.

8

ANA Intercontinental
(www.anaintercontinental-tokyo.jp/e/)
1-12-44 Akasaka, Minato-ku, Tokyo 107-0052
Tel: 81-3-3505-1111
Fax: 81-3-3505-1155
E-mail: info@anaintercontinental-tokyo.jp

Conveniently located in the Ark Hills complex (which also houses the magnificent Suntory Concert Hall), the ANA Intercontinental is just a matter of minutes away from Kasumigaseki, the seat of Japan's government and also from Roppongi, one of the city's busiest entertainment districts. It offers a wide range of rooms and a good selection of bars and restaurants as well as a fitness centre. The Business Centre can help with translations and the preparation of business cards and has meeting space available for hotel guests.

The Conrad Tokyo
(http://tokyo.conradmeetings.com/)
1-9-1 Higashi-Shinbashi, Minato-Ku, Tokyo 105-7377
Tel: 81-3-6388-8000
Fax: 81 3-6388-8001
E-mail: tokyoinfo@conradhotels.com

The Conrad is located in Shiodome, one of the city's more recent high-rise developments. It is within walking distance of the Ginza, the prestigious shopping and entertainment district and affords splendid panoramic views of the Tokyo Bay and of the Hamarikyu Garden, a former imperial residence. It has the largest spa facility of any of the capital's hotels and is also home to the restaurant Gordon Ramsay – the first Asian venture by the UK's three-star Michelin chef.

The Grand Hyatt
(http://tokyo.grand.hyatt.com/)
6-10-3 Roppongi, Minato-Ku, Tokyo, 106-0032
Tel: 81-3-4333-1234
Fax: 81-3-4333-8123
E-mail: tokyo.grand@hyatt.com

This luxury five-star hotel is located in the heart of one of the city's main entertainment districts and is part of Roppongi Hills, the capital's largest private urban

8

redevelopment project that is made up of office space, private accommodation, a cinema complex, shopping facilities and the Mori Art Museum. The hotel also hosts the Nagomi Spa and Fitness Centre and a broad selection of bars and restaurants. Of these, the French Kitchen is very popular among foreign residents of the city.

The Hilton Tokyo

(www1.hilton.com/en_US/hi/hotel/TYOHITW-Hilton-Tokyo-hotel/index.do)
6-2 Nishi-Shinjuku 6-chome, Shinjuku-Ku, Tokyo 160-0023
Tel: 81-3-3344-5111
Fax: 81-3-3342-6094
E-mail: tokyo@hilton.com

Following a three year multi-million dollar refurbishment the Hilton Tokyo now has one of the finest Executive Floors in the city and an impressive selection of bars and restaurants. There is a complimentary shuttle bus service between the hotel and Shinjuku station and the Oedo Subway Line is directly accessible through an underground passageway.

The Imperial Hotel

(www.imperialhotel.co.jp)
1-1, Uchisaiwai-cho 1-chome, Chiyoda-ku, Tokyo 100-8558, Japan
Tel: 81-3-3504-1111/(Reservation) 81-3-3504-1251
Fax: 81-3-3581-9146/(Reservation) 81-3-3504-1258

The original Imperial Hotel – a wooden structure – was founded in 1890 at the command of the Imperial Palace. In 1923, a striking new stone extension built by Frank Lloyd Wright opened and remained in business until 1968 when it was declared no longer safe and a new hotel was built on the original site. Part of the Frank Lloyd Wright building has been reconstructed in Meiji Mura outside Nagoya and today's Imperial Hotel is home to the Old Imperial Bar which is in the Lloyd Wright style and a favourite watering hole among many expat residents. The Imperial is where you will also find "Les Saisons", long regarded as one of Tokyo's finest French restaurants.

8

The Imperial today retains a classic elegance but is equipped with the latest technology. The Executive Service Centre is the largest of its kind in Japan, occupying an entire wing of the 5th floor of the Main Building. It is centrally located next to Hibiya Park and within a short walk of the Imperial Palace and surrounding moat.

The New Otani
(www.newotani.co.jp/en/tokyo/)
4-1 Kioi-cho, Chiyoda-ku, Tokyo 102-8578
Tel: 81-3-3265-1111
Fax: 81-3-3221-2619

Fans of James Bond may recognise the New Otani Tower as the HQ of Osato Chemicals in 1967's "You Only Live Twice". Opened in 1964 in time for the Tokyo Olympic Games, the hotel has recently been completely renovated. It is very centrally located and yet houses an oasis of calm. The 400-year old Japanese garden is one of the most renowned in Tokyo and spreads over ten acres. It is surrounded by the outer moat of the historic Edo Castle, and is rich in foliage of all kinds. There are also carp ponds and an attractive waterfall. Some of the hotel restaurants are in the garden. The New Otani is also the home to two unique restaurants.

Trader Vics is an informal bar and restaurant with a South Pacific theme and which on Sundays offers an all-you-can-eat brunch accompanied by free-flowing sparkling wine for a very reasonable ¥6,000 (US$60/€44) per head. If you are really lucky you may find yourself at a table with a great view over the Japanese garden and waterfall. General Manager Larry Murakami is a most congenial host and has made TVs a favourite spot among foreign residents of Tokyo.

La Tour d'Argent, on the other hand, is for those with a more formal approach to dining and with a serious expense account. The only "branch" of the 400-year old Parisian restaurant most famous for its pressed duck, La Tour d'Argent in the New Otani has a very impressive menu and a superb wine list. Dinner starts at ¥21,000 (US$210/€154) without wines, tax and service.

The Mandarin Oriental
(www.mandarinoriental.com/tokyo)
2-1-1 Nihonbashi Muromachi, Chuo-ku, Tokyo, 103-8328
Tel: +81-3-3270-8800
E-mail: motyo-reservations@mohg.com

Located in Nihonbashi, a matter of minutes away from the Tokyo Stock Exchange, the Mandarin Oriental sits atop the tallest tower in the area and offers spectacular views across the city. It is close to Tokyo Station and the Ginza Line subway can be directly accessed from the basement level of the hotel. The Mandarin Oriental claims that its rooms are some of the most spacious in the city. It offers a spa and business centre and a variety of restaurants.

The Hotel Okura
(www.okura.com/tokyo/)
2-10-4 Toranomon, Minato-ku, Tokyo 105-0001
Tel: + 81-3-3582-0111
Fax: +81-3-3582-3707

The Okura is a Tokyo institution; there are many regular visitors to Japan who will stay nowhere else, drawn back by the calm professionalism of the staff and the discrete service offered. At a time when many of the city's hotels strive for the dramatic, the Okura remains true to its mission of providing reliable service, whether in-room or in one of the several bars and restaurants. The Highlander Bar is popular with foreign residents of Tokyo, too. The Okura is located in the immediate vicinity of the Spanish, Swedish and US Embassies.

The Park Hyatt
(www.tokyo.park.hyatt.com/hyatt/hotels/index.jsp)
3-7-1-2 Nishi Shinjuku, Tokyo 163-1055
Tel: +81-3-5322-1234 Fax: +81-3-5322-1288
E-mail: Tokyo.park@hyatt.com

Located on the top 14 floors of the 52-storey Shinjuku Park Tower, the Park Hyatt was famously the location for Sofia Coppola's 2003 hit movie "Lost in Translation". Close to Shinjuku Station – the busiest in the world in terms of passenger useage; an average of 3.5

8

million a day in 2007 – the hotel is on the western side which is very business-oriented. The eastern side of the station tends to be more focused on shopping and entertainment, with at least one area that is decidedly seedy and not to be recommended. The hotel's best known restaurant, The New York Grill, sits on the 52nd floor with floor-to-ceiling glass windows offering breathtaking views of Tokyo (if you have a head for heights; acrophobics beware!). There's a Big Apple décor and a wine cellar of over 1500 bottles.

The Peninsula

(www.peninsula.com/tokyo/en/default.aspx)
1-8-1 Yurakucho, Chiyoda-ku, Tokyo 100-0006
Tel: +81-3-6270-2888
Fax: +81-3-6270-2000
E-mail: ptk@peninsula.com

This five star luxury hotel has a prime location, immediately opposite the Imperial Palace and the surrounding gardens and a matter of a few minutes walk to the Ginza shopping and entertainment district. The Peninsula has some of the most spacious rooms in the city and offers a variety of cuisines in addition to a traditional afternoon tea that is served in the lobby and which is extremely popular with well-heeled Japanese ladies of a certain age and position in life.

The Ritz Carlton

(www.ritzcarlton.com/en/Properties/Tokyo/Default.htm)
Tokyo Midtown, 9-7-1, Akasaka, Minato-ku, Tokyo 107-6245
Tel: +81-3-3423-8000
Fax: +81-3-3423-8001

The hotel occupies the first three levels and the top nine floors of the 53-storey Midtown Tower – for the time being the capital's tallest building. Its emphasis is on superior service, ensuring that guests have a totally satisfactory experience such that they will want to return.

The Westin Tokyo
1-4-1 Mita, Meguro-ku, Tokyo 153-8580
Tel: +81-3-5423-7000
Fax: +81-3-5423-7600
(www.starwoodhotels.com/westin/property/overview/ind
ex.html?propertyID=1062)

The Westin is connected by a covered walkway to Ebisu
Station on the Yamanote and Hibiya Subway lines. This
is an area once famous for brewing Yebisu Beer which is
named after the Japanese god of fishermen, good luck
and good health; one of Japan's Seven Gods of Fortune.
The hotel is decorated in a European style and features
what it styles Heavenly Beds®.

Budget hotels

8

Should your travel budget not extend to the hotels listed
above, the city also has a range of slightly less expensive
accommodation that is nonetheless perfectly respectable
and where you can still count on reliable and efficient
service. For example, there are a number of hotels run
by the Tokyu Group (which also operates busses, trains
and department stores) under the name Excel.
See the website at:
www.tokyuhotelsjapan.com/en/area/kanto.html.

There is also a good listing of moderately priced hotels at:
http://gojapan.about.com/cs/tokyoaccom/l/bltokyo_modi
dx.htm.

A note on tax and service at hotels

All hotels and *ryokan* (inns) in Japan will add a 5%
consumption tax to your final bill. Additionally there
will be a service charge of between 10-15%. In Tokyo
itself there is also a very small (¥100 – 200) "Tokyo
Accommodation Charge". Remember, however, that you
do not tip in Japan and that applies to restaurants and
taxis as well. Indeed, in certain circumstances, offering a
gratuity could cause offence since people in the service
and hospitality business in Japan take great professional
pride in giving their best; to tip them is considered
condescending.

Where to eat

It is estimated that there are something like 10,000 restaurants in Tokyo, ranging from tiny noodle shops to the most sophisticated establishments selling just about every kind of cuisine from all over the world. In 2007 Michelin confirmed the city's culinary standing with the publication of their first Guide to restaurants in Tokyo, awarding a total of 191 stars (by contrast Paris has 98 and London just 50).

So when it comes to wining and dining, Tokyo has a great deal to offer over and above the international kitchens of its fine hotels. It is true that for some of them you need seriously deep pockets (and don't assume that your credit card will be accepted, especially in the upper-end traditional Japanese restaurants: check when you make your reservation) but the good news is that you can eat really well in Tokyo at very reasonable prices. Many restaurants offer special lunch-time set menus that are not much more expensive than the average fast-food outlet. But a word of caution: the same restaurant may well prove to be much less reasonably priced in the evenings. Much depends on location.

It would be futile to try and give a comprehensive list of suggested places to eat, so what follows is a very personal selection of some of the less obvious places that have proved to be reliable and of good value. They are largely places suited to social entertaining rather than strict business meetings, though none are inappropriate. A good place to gain a more complete overview of all that is on offer by area is the website www.jselect.net/wd/. You can also buy a hard copy of the same guide, "Wining and Dining in Tokyo", in most hotel bookshops for less than ¥1,000 (US$10.-/€8.-). One of the most useful things about the printed guide (which is regularly updated) is that it provides very good maps in English.

So, in no particular order, some suggestions:

Queen Sheba (Ethiopian)
B1 Neoage Nakameguro Bldg. 1-3-1 Higashiyama, Meguro-ku Tokyo 153-0061
Tel: 03-3794-1801

(A 7-minute walk from Nakameguro station on the Hibiya Subway Line)

Not the first cuisine you'd think about when visiting Japan but owner-chef Solomon has created a truly authentic Ethiopian experience, both in terms of décor and atmosphere and with a stunning menu. There is also an amazing range of African beers and other exotic drinks and there's live blues on the first Tuesday and third Sunday of each month. The staff are friendly and the prices extremely reasonable. Not in the centre-most part of town, but definitely worth the effort to get there. This is a good, friendly place to relax if you are dining alone.

Ninja (Japanese)
Akasaka Tokyu Plaza, 2-14-3 Nagatacho, Chiyoda-ku, Tokyo 100-0014
Tel: (03) 5157-3936
(At Akasakamitsuke station on the Ginza and Marunouchi Subway Lines)

8

This has to be one of the most unusual restaurants in town. Dining at Ninja is quite an experience, beginning right from the minute you ask to be admitted (and you won't be if you haven't made reservations). There are trap doors, secret panels, drawbridges and all manner of obstacles to overcome before – escorted by an appropriately costumed Ninja – you reach your table. Most are in private booths (it's not the sort of place you dine alone in) and your evening will include some pretty impressive close-up magic right at your table. The menu offers a variety of mainly Japanese dishes and you can order set courses or à la carte. It is not cheap, but remember you're also paying for the entertainment value of the setting and the performers. Not recommended if you're intent is to negotiate a contract over dinner; it's nevertheless a good place to have fun when you celebrate having signed one.

Bistro Bonne Femme (French)
Tameike Suzuki Bldg., Akasaka 1-3-13, Minato-ku
Tokyo 107-0052
Tel: (03) - 3582-0200

(A 10 minute walk from Tameike-Sanno Station or Roppongi 1-chome Station on the Namboku Subway Line or Kokkai-Gijidomae Station on the Chiyoda and Ginza Subway Lines)

This is an understated gem of a restaurant in the immediate vicinity of the US Embassy, serving up classic French dishes at very reasonable prices. Maître Minami-san speaks English and French with consummate ease and the service is discrete and professional. It's a good choice for a business lunch or dinner. Set menus are available for both and there is an impressive à la carte selection. Rumour has it, Bonne Femme serves the finest crème brûlée in Asia.

Elio Locanda (Italian)
Hanzomon House 203, Kojimachi, 2-5-2 Chiyoda-ku, Tokyo 102-0083
Tel: (03)-3239-6771
(7 minutes from Kojimachi station on the Yurakucho Subway Line or Hanzomon station on the Hanzomon Line)

Restaurateur Elio Osara has been a chef most of his life. A native of Calabria, Elio brings to Tokyo the very best of Southern Italian food, rich with influences from Spain, Greece and Sicily. Only the freshest of ingredients and the finest of wines are good enough for this Cavaliere della Repubblica d'Italia, and Elio and his staff (both Italian and Japanese) manage to make every customer feel as if they're the most important they've ever served. Prices are very reasonable, especially at lunchtime, the waiters are very happy to explain whatever seasonal special is on offer and the kitchen is very flexible when it comes to accommodating special dietary needs. A hugely popular venue not far from the British Embassy – the President of Italy in 1999 certified it Japan's best Italian restaurant – it is advisable to book well ahead. Tables tend to be close together, so it's not ideal for business conversations that may be sensitive.

Nanbantei (Japanese)
Roppongi 4-5-6, Minato-ku Tokyo 106-0032
Tel: (03) 3402-0606
(8 minutes walk from Roppongi Station on the Hibiya and Oedo Subway Lines)

An intimate and traditionally styled restaurant a short walk from the Roppongi crossing, Nanbantei serves *yakitori*, charcoal grilled chicken, offal and vegetables on skewers. These are eaten with salt and lemon juice or a dip called *tare*, consisting of *sake*, *mirin*, soy sauce and sugar (though each restaurant jealously guards the exact make up its *tare* receipe). It's possible to order piece by piece, but the simpler (and more cost effective) way is to order one of the set menus. Nanbantei has a menu in English and some of the staff speak English well enough to help you make the most of your visit. Reservations strongly recommended. Unusually, the restaurant is closed on Saturdays.

Nobu Tokyo (Japanese-fusion)
1F Toranomon Tower Office, 4-1-28 Toranomon, Minato-ku, Tokyo 105-0001
Tel: 03-5733-0070

8

(10-12 minutes walk from Roppongi 1-chome Station and Temeike Sanno Station on the Namboku Subway Line, Kamiyacho Station on the Hibiya Subway Line, and Toranomon Station on the Ginza Subway Line)

Owner-chef Nobuyuki Matsuhisa is known for blending traditional Japanese dishes with Peruvian and Argentine ingredients. Like his other restaurants in other parts of the world, the Tokyo venue is co-owned by Robert De Niro. It is a modern, trendy dining spot with a pleasant bar area and an interesting menu offering dishes that are not particularly expensive. There is also a separate sushi bar. The restaurant is in the tower block immediately behind the South Wing of the Hotel Okura. Reservations are essential.

Suji's (New York Korean)
Azabudai Hinoki Bldg 1st F, 3-1-5 Azabudai, Minato-ku, Tokyo 106,0041
Tel: 03-3505-4490
(12 minutes walk from Roppongi Station on the Hibiya Subway Line or from Roppongi 1-chome on the Namboku Subway Line)

This is a relative newcomer to the Tokyo scene but has already made a sharp impression. Owner Suji Park has created an appealling casual space, including a small outside terrace, where the staff are friendly and the food is really interesting. This is one of the few affordable places in town where the vegetarian offerings are truly creative and tempting enough for non-vegetarians to want to sample them.

The Taj (Indian)
1F. Koei Bldg. 2-7, Akasaka 3-chome, Minato-ku, Tokyo 107-0052
Tel: 03-3586-6606
(A 3 minute walk from Akasakamitsuke Station on the Ginza, Marunouchi, and Hanzomon Subway Lines)

Though there are now countless Indian restaurants in Tokyo, The Taj is seen by many to be the most authentic. It's been in business since 1975 and under the careful management of Mr Roy serves consistently good food at extremely reasonable prices. Unlike many Indian restaurants in the city, it is not part of a chain and it is not a small hole-in-the-wall operation; the Taj can accommodate over 100 people.

Sukiyabashi Jiro   (Sushi)
Address: 2-15, Ginza 4-chome, Chuo-ku, Tokyo
(Tsukamoto Bld. B1F)
Tel: 03-3535-3600

There are many excellent sushi restaurants in the Shimbashi-Ginza area. Jiro is particularly in focus right now for having been awarded 3 Michelin stars. It is a very small restaurant and extremely popular, so reserve well ahead of time. If you are not concerned with what the final bill will be, let Jiro serve you what he feels is the best of the day's catch; choice pieces of the fish he himself will have selected that morning at the Tsukiji fish market.

Casual Dining (California)
The celebrated chef Wolfgang Puck (who's Spago was for several years one of the hottest spots in Tokyo) now has a number of more casual and less expensive outlets offering California Cuisine. These are relaxed places where the food is good, the wine reliable if not exciting, and the prices very reasonable indeed (especially at

lunchtime). Details of the cafés are at: www.wp-japan.jp/shop/index.html.

Drinks

There is no shortage of watering holes in Tokyo. They range from the simplest aka-chochin (red lantern) *sake* bars to the most sophisticated cocktail bars in the major hotels. You may, if you are lucky, be taken by your Japanese contacts to some of the exclusive hostess bars in the Ginza and such areas but it is not advisable for the foreign business traveller to try and enter and negotiate these alone. Many are by introduction- or member-only and they can be extremely expensive indeed. Should you be invited to such a place, please do not misunderstand the meaning of the word "hostess". One small tip: if you do not wish to drink anymore, leave your glass full. Each time you drink from it, it will be replenished. Trying to stop someone refilling your glass is considered rude; you are refusing hospitality. Leaving your glass full is a polite way of saying enough's enough.

Alternatively, you may wish to invite your Japanese contacts to something altogether different. The city is studded with "British Pubs" and "Irish Bars" serving pub-style meals and a variety of imported beers and other drinks. Some of these style themselves "sports bars" and offer wide hi-vision monitors screening a variety of sporting events such as soccer, rugby and baseball. Great fun if you want to relax but not the place to go for a business discussion.

Some of the names to watch out for:

Hobgoblin: www.hobgoblin.jp/
HUB:www.englishok.jp/shops/hub/
Paddy Foley's: www.paddyfoleystokyo.com/
Dubliners:
http://ultimatepubguide.com/pubs/info.phtml?pub_id=316
The Rose & Crown:
www.englishok.jp/shops/pubs_bars/british/rose-and-crown/akasaka/

A good source of information on the newest places to wine and dine are the various "freebie" newspapers and

8

magazines that are published in English. The finest of these is the "Weekender" but there are others such as "Metropolis" and they are normally available in hotels and other places where foreigners are likely to gather.

9

other places
of interest

other places
of interest

While it is true that the majority of business travellers will find themselves concentrating on Tokyo, there are other centres of activity that may be of interest, depending on the business sector that is of most concern. What follows is a brief overview of some of the most important ones. It must be noted that hotel and restaurant listings are simply representative; they are not intended to be all-embracing. You can find much more information at www.japan-guide.com.

• Aichi Prefecture

Aichi is literally in the heartland of Japan and forms a bridge between the nation's eastern and western cultures. Its capital city is Nagoya with a population of some 2.24 million[1] making it the country's third largest incorporated city. The area is strong in manufacturing, both in the traditional areas of textiles and ceramics but, more importantly in the high tech industries: aerospace, machine tools and, especially, automobiles. This is where Japan's automotive giant Toyota has its corporate headquarters and the area is strongly identified with the name. There is even a Toyota City. In 2007 the value of manufactured goods shipped from Aichi represented 13.3% of the national total[2].

9

Since 2005, when Nagoya hosted the World Exposition, the region has had its own 24-hour international airport (Centrair – the Central Japan International Airport) which offers easy access to Nagoya by rail, road and sea. The city is roughly half way between Tokyo and Osaka and has recently seen significant urban redevelopment in the centre with high rise buildings springing up with some regularity. There are also plans to develop a base facility that will support industry and international business, though few specifics have been announced to date.

Like most other Japanese urban centres, Nagoya is well served when it comes to public transport. There are a number of train and subway lines and a city-wide bus service that operates on a flat fee basis (¥200).

---

[1] 2007. Source; Aichi International Association
[2] Source: Aichi International Association

Hotels in Nagoya

The Hilton Hotel

1-3-3 Sakae Naka-ku Nagoya, Aichi , Japan 460-0008
Tel: +81-52-212-1111
Fax: +81-52-212-1225

A five star hotel very conveniently located for both
the airport and the business centre and featuring the
"Windows on the World" bar and restaurant.

The Meitetsu Grand Hotel

Meieki 1-chome, Nakamura-ku, Nagoya, Aichi, Japan
450-0002
Tel: +81-52-582-2211
Fax: +81-52-582-2230

Another five star hotel that is located immediately next
to Nagoya's main station offering good business support
services and classic Japanese hospitality.

The Westin Nagoya Castle Hotel

3-19 Hinokuchi-cho, Nishi-ku Nagoya, Aichi Japan 451-
8551
Tel: +81-52-521 2121
Fax: +81-52-531-3313

This four star hotel is located immediately in front of
Nagoya's historic Castle yet affords all the most modern
amenities in its business centre and spa. Also on offer,
the Westin chain's signature Heavenly Beds®

Where to eat in Nagoya

Sawasdee Sumiyoshi   *(Thai)*

3-11-12 Chiyoda Naka-ku Nagoya, Aichi, Japan 460-
0012
Tel: +81-52-332-3639

Thai food is very popular in Japan but sometimes
restaurants adjust the ingredients to make their dishes
more appealing to local palates. Not so here, where the
chefs are as genuinely Thai as the décor and the items on
the menu are as authentic as any in Bangkok. Not for
those with a low tolerance for spices.

Shige Yakitori Dining Bar *(Japanese)*
3-2-30 Sakae, Naka-ku, Nagoya, Aichi Japan 460-0008
Tel: +81-52-241-9881

Definitely not your average chicken on skewers type
place, Shige uses the meat of specially reared chickens
and offers six different sauces to complement the grilled
meats. The atmosphere has a kind of New York feel to it.

Gira Sole   *(Italian)*
5-1097-1 Higashi Ozone-cho Naka-ku, Nagoya, Aichi
Japan 461-0022
Tel: +81-52-911-8335

Reputed to be the finest Italian restaurant in the city,
Gira Sole offers an extensive selection of fish and seafood
delicacies, meats and an assortment of pizza and pasta
dishes. There is an extensive wine list including some
first rate Italian regional wines.

Yamamotoya Sohonke   *(Japanese)*
3-12-19 Sakae, Naka-ku, Nagoya, Aichi, Japan 460-0008
Tel: +81-52-241-5617

Traditional Nagoya cuisine uses a lot of miso (a paste
made from soy beans) and a firm favourite is nikomi
udon, a dish of thick chewy noodles and other
ingredients in a rich tasty broth made of two types of
miso. This restaurant has been in business since 1925
and it claims the taste of its nikomi udon has remained
entirely unchanged all this time. It's also said that if you
eat it there three times you will become addicted to
the dish.

Urbana Latina   *(Brazilian)*
Koasa Bldg. B1F, 4-2-10 Sakae, Naka-ku, Nagoya, Aichi
Japan 460-0008
Tel: +81-52-252-0127

A century ago there was large-scale emigration
from Japan to Brazil. A significant number of the
grandchildren of the original émigrés have chosen
to return to Japan, many of them settling in Aichi
Prefecture to raise their families there (in fact Toyota
City claims that roughly 50 percent of its population is

of Japanese Brazilian descent). So it's not surprising to find a truly authentic Brazilian restaurant in Nagoya. There's a varied menu, a rich selection of drinks and a quartet of Brazilian musicians to set your feet tapping.

●   Fukuoka Prefecture

Fukuoka Prefecture is often called the gateway to Asia because of its location at the northernmost part of Kyushu, the southernmost of the four main Japanese islands. Its two international airports allow business travellers to reach parts of the Asian region within a matter of a couple of hours, with even day trips to Seoul, Shanghai and Taipei easily manageable. The population of the Prefecture – a little over 5 million – puts it ahead of Norway and Sweden, while the population of Kyushu itself is 15 million, putting it ahead of Belgium, Hong Kong and Denmark .

9

There are two major ports in the Prefecture, Hakata and Kitakyushu, which both rank among the top facilities in the world in terms of volume of container traffic. As with the rest of the island, Fukuoka enjoys a well developed network of highways and rail connections. The Prefecture boasts 36 universities, eleven of which specialize in science and engineering, and attracts a large number of foreign students, in part because of the pleasant living environment and significantly lower cost of living than that in Tokyo or Osaka for example.

Fukuoka has been very aggressive in encouraging foreign direct investment and in promoting what it terms "next-generation industries":

Automotive
Biotechnology
Environmental Technology
Hydrogen Energy
Information and Communication Technology
Multimedia
Nanotechnology
Robotics

[3] Fukuoka Foreign Investment Promotion Centre

You can find further details of these nine sectors by
visiting www.investfk.jp.

ANA Hotel Hakata
3-3-3 Hakata Ekimae, Hakata-ku Fukuoka-shi,
Fukuoka-en, Japan 812 0011
Tel: +81-92-471-7111
Fax: +81-92-471-1109

A five star hotel located right by the main railway
station. There is an indoor fitness centre and pool.

Hotel Okura
Hakata Riverain 3-2 Shimokawabata-machi Hakata-ku,
Fukuoka Japan 812-0027
Tel: +81-92-262-1111
Fax: +81-92-262-7701

Okura service is recognised as amongst the best in the
industry and you'll find it in this five star hotel in droves.
Well-appointed rooms and fine bars and dining are a
given. The hotel is in the same development as the city's
Asian Arts Museum.

The New Otani Hakata
1-1-2 Watanabe-dori, Chuo-ku, Fukuoka-shi, Fukuoka-
ken, Japan 810-0004
Tel: +81-92-714-1111
Fax: +81-92-715-5658

A four star hotel well known for its fine service and
friendly staff. Conveniently located and well equipped
to meet the business traveller's needs.

One of the symbols of Fukuoka City is its open air food
stalls (known as *yatai*). You will find them all over the
city but especially in the central areas. They typically are
open from around 6 pm and, depending on the weather,
will stay open until 2 am. They serve such dishes as
yakitori (chicken grilled on skewers), *ramen* (thin
noodles in a pork broth) *oden* (a kind of hot pot) and
gyoza (dumplings). Beer, *sake* (rice wine), and *shochu* (a
kind of Japanese vodka) are also served. Eating at a *yatai*

9

is a great way to sample the real Fukuoka and to meet the friendly Fukuokans. Other than that:

Ichiran Ramen Restaurant   *(Japanese)*
1-10-15 Tenjin, Chuo-ku, Fukuoka City, Fukuoka Prefecture, Japan 810-0001

Fukuoka is famous for its literally hundreds of restaurants serving *ramen* – noodles in broth with various toppings such as leeks, pork, bean sprouts and so on. Ichiran is a favourite of many of Fukuoka's foreign residents. It's informal (no reservations) and inexpensive and has a very extensive selection of *ramen* dishes.

Aburayama Sanso Restaurant   *(Japanese)*
147 Higashi-Aburayama, Jonan-ku, Fukuoka City, Fukuoka Prefecture, Japan 814-0155
Tel: +81-92-871-5034

Fukuoka is very well known for its fine fish and shellfish. One dish in particular is closely associated with the city – *fugu* (puffer fish). Only chefs who are licensed to do so may serve this dish because the livers of certain fish contain a deadly poison. There are numerous *fugu* restaurants in Fukuoka but this one is slightly different in that it is out of the city centre and offers a truly Japanese atmosphere and décor. A meal here will not be cheap but it will be a special experience. Prior reservations are essential as it is extremely popular.

Tundra   *(Russian)*
2-7-11 Daimyo, Chuo-ku, Fukuoka City, Fukuoka Prefecture, Japan 810-0041
Tel: +81-92-751-7028

This friendly and very popular (since 1960) restaurant is not for those with small appetites. Here you'll find dishes designed to help you survive a Russian winter. In fairness, however, the restaurant does also offer a variety of items for the health-conscious.

Il Boccone *(Italian)*
2-4-1 Keiko, Chuo-ku, Fukuoka City, Fukuoka Prefecture, Japan 810-0001
Tel: +81-92-731-1536

Advertising itself as "Italian with a twist" this casual restaurant serves up a variety of traditional dishes but with imaginative differences so that a meal eaten here will be quite unique. The chef grows all his own vegetables and herbs and insists on only the freshest of ingredients.

• Osaka Prefecture

Osaka Prefecture is right at the centre of Japan and is made up of 33 cities, 9 towns and one village. Its capital is the City of Osaka. Though it is one of the smaller Prefectures, Osaka's total population is 8.8 million, making it the third most populous in the country after Tokyo and Kanagawa[4]. The Prefecture's GDP is roughly the same as Switzerland's.

The region has long been known as a mercantile centre as well as a driving force in the country's industrial development. Something like 65% of all SMEs involved in manufacturing in Japan are Osaka-based and many export their home-grown technology around the world. In 2006 "Newsweek" announced its global 500 top companies in terms of financial performance and Corporate Social Responsibility. Nineteen of those companies were headquartered in Osaka, including Takeda Pharmaceuticals and Matsushita Electric[5].

The City of Osaka itself has a resident population of a little over 2.6 million (though the daytime population rises to 3.6 million) and has a GDP of US$213 billion, exceeding that of Hong Kong. The City is currently focused on the redevelopment of a large area north of the main Station and has ambitious plans for even larger scale urban regeneration, including a face-lift for the Midosuji District. It is also concentrating on some key industrial sectors, among them robotics[6], healthcare and preventative medicines and Ubiquitous Network Technology.

9

[4] Source: Osaka Prefectural Government
[5] Source Newsweek June 2006
[6] See Chapter Six

Osaka

Access to Osaka is very convenient. Shin-Osaka station is one of the key stops on the Tokaido Shinkansen (Bullet Train) Line and there are two airports: Osaka International Airport (which, confusingly, is domestic) and Kansai International Airport.

Hotels in Osaka

Nikko Hotel
1-3-3 Nishi-Shinsaibashi, Chuo-ku, Osaka City, Osaka Prefecture, 542-0086 Japan
Tel: +81-6-6244-1111
Fax: +81-6-6245-2432

---

[7]Sometimes now called Itami Airport

Conveniently located across from the tree-lined Mido-Suji avenue, this 5 star hotel is within walking distance of the main business district as well as the leading entertainment district. It has a number of restaurants and bars, including the Sky Liner on the 31st floor. There is also an indoor pool.

The Ritz-Carlton Hotel
2-5-25 Umeda, Kita-ku, Osaka City, Osaka Prefecture, 530-0001 Japan
Tel: +81-6-6343-7000
Fax: +81-6-6343-7001

A name that is synonymous with service, this 5 star hotel is just moments away from Osaka's main railway station and close to several bars and restaurants. Naturally the hotel offers its own, from traditional Japanese through classic French, to informal Italian. There is also a business centre that is open 24 hours.

The Westin Hotel
1-1-20 Oyodonaka, Kita-ku, Osaka City, Osaka Prefecture 531-0076 Japan
Tel: +81-6-6440-1111
Fax: +81-6-6440-1100

The first Westin in Japan, this 4 star hotel is located in Shin Umeda City about a 10 minute walk from Osaka's central station. This newly developing urban area is especially known for the sky garden in the Umeda Sky Building. The Westin Osaka offers a good selection of bars and restaurants, including the "Imperial Palace" serving classic Cantonese cuisine.

Where to eat in Osaka
Osaka has long been known as *Tenka-no-Daidokoro* (The Nation's Kitchen) and over the years has developed a unique culinary culture. You would have to spend a good deal longer than the average business trip to be able to sample all the different kinds of dishes that are on offer. Here are a few ideas to get you started.

Okonomiyaki Madonna *(Japanese)*
1-88 Umeda, Kita-ku, Osaka City, Osaka Prefecture 530-0001 Japan
Tel: +81-6-6347-7371

9

Okonomiyaki is particularly popular in the Kansai. It is a pancake-like dish made from cabbage, flour, pork, shrimp and whatever other ingredients may come to hand, grilled on a hot plate and covered with a rich sauce. In many places the customer is encouraged to make his own. This casual restaurant in the basement of the building next to the Hilton Hotel is perfect for someone dining alone, and has very friendly and helpful staff.

Kani Dotonbori   *(Japanese)*
1-6-18 Dotonbori, Chuo-ku, Osaka City, Osaka Prefecture 542-0071 Japan
Tel: +81-6-6211-8975

You simply can't miss this restaurant because it has a gigantic mechanical crab waving its legs and claws about above the entrance. The restaurant serves crab (*kani*) in an astonishing variety of ways, from sushi to salad, roasted and fried; even crab sukiyaki. This is the main location (there are over 50 around Japan) and the largest, having several floors.

La Bamba del Rio *(Mexican)*
2-3-23 Dotonbori, Chuo-ku, Osaka City, Osaka Prefecture, 542-0071 Japan
Tel: +81-6-6213-9612

This is a small but brightly decorated restaurant offering cheerful service and the usual Mexican assortment of tacos, enchiladas and so on, as well as the drinks to go with them.

Jafance   *(French)*
1-1-27 Shibata, Kita-ku, Osaka City, Osaka Prefecture, 530-0012 Japan
Tel: +81-6-6372-7667

The name says it all, a bringing together of Japan and France. The restaurant serves up a variety of classic French dishes and while there is a very good wine cellar, diners are often encouraged to try matching the food with Japanese sake. There's a good a la carte selection but the set menus are also a very good choice.

9

Sorubiba   *(Organic)*
6-12-20 Minami Semba, Chuo-ku, Osaka City, Osaka
Prefecture, 542-0081 Japan
Tel: +81-6-6253-0175

A charming restaurant with a Mediterranean feel and
an outdoor terrace. The chef uses only the finest organic
ingredients and while there are plenty of meat and fish
dishes on the menu, which changes daily, there is always
a good selection of vegetarian options.

● Yokohama

Yokohama (the capital city of Kanagawa Prefecture) is a
mere 30 kilometers south of Tokyo but it has a character
all of its own. Japan's second largest city – and busiest
port – it has a long tradition of being international in
flavour. It was one of the first ports to be opened to
foreign trade in the late 19th Century. Trade in silk was
important to the emerging economy and the biggest
trader was Great Britain. The British were instrumental
in developing Yokohama in other areas, too; one British
merchant created the city's first coal-burning power
plant and British railway engineers created the first link
between Yokohama and Shimbashi Station in Tokyo.
Once a small fishing village, Yokohama now has a
population of more than 3.6 million, making it the
second most populous city in Japan after Tokyo.

9

Like Tokyo, Yokohama suffered greatly at the time of
the Great Kanto Earthquake of 1923 and was again
severely damaged during the air raids of the Pacific War.
It quickly recovered and is today a dynamic centre with
its own distinct personality.

Hotels in Yokohama

InterContinental Yokohama The Grand
1-1-1 Minatomirai, Nishi-ku, Yokohama City,
Kanagawa Prefecture 220-8522 Japan 1-1-2
Tel: +81-45-223-2222
Fax: +81-45-221-0650

This striking 5 star hotel sits right on the waterfront but
is a matter of minutes away from Yokohama Station. It
is located in an area where there is a major convention

9

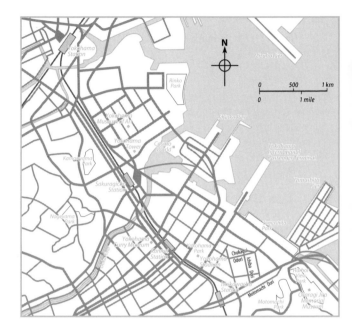

Yokohama

and conference centre, a number of shopping malls and some interesting attractions, including the celebrated Red Brick Warehouses (Akarenga Soko). Originally built as customs houses, these have been beautifully restored and now house shops, galleries and restaurants. The hotel itself offers all you would expect from a first class InterContinental, including free airport transfers.

Yokohama Royal Park Hotel
2-2-1-3 Minatomirai, Nishi-ku, Yokohama City, Kanagawa Prefecture 220-8173 Japan
Tel: +81-45-221-1111
Fax: +81-45-224-5153

This 5 star hotel occupies the 49th – 70th floors of what is currently Japan's tallest building, the Landmark Tower, and offers unsurpassed views across the Yokohama Bay Bridge and beyond it, Mt Fuji. Meticulous attention to detail and a friendly and helpful staff have earned the Royal Park a reputation that is well deserved. Minatomirai itself is Yokohama's showpiece – a city within a city where you will find plenty to occupy your time and your imagination.

Yokohama Excel Tokyu
1-1-12 Minamisaiwai, Nishi-ku, Yokohama City, Kanagawa Prefecture 220-0005
Tel: +81-45-311-1682
Fax: +81-45-311-1084

Well suited to the business traveller on a limited budget (apart from anything else, it offers free internet connections), this somewhat older hotel is right by the West Exit of Yokohama Station. The rooms tend to be small but the service is all that you would expect from the Tokyu Group. There's plenty of shopping nearby and the celebrated Chinatown is a 10 minute subway ride away.

9

Where to eat in Yokohama

Without a doubt Chinatown is a must. As soon as Yokohama was opened to the outside world, Chinese traders were quick to take advantage and to settle here. Today, Chinatown is a thriving, colourful community of shops and restaurants offering everything from simple snacks to elaborate banquets. Many of the restaurants are very small with just a handful of tables. You turn up and take your place in the queue. Others are more sophisticated. A recent development is the Yokohama Daisekai (known locally as *Daska*). This is a sort of food theme park that seeks to re-create the Shanghai of the 1920s. More than a dozen food stalls offer a variety of dishes, some prepared by Shanghai's most reputable restaurants.

Sitar   *(Indian)*
74-6 Yamashita-cho, Naka-ku, Yokohama City, Kanagawa Prefecture 231-0023 Japan
Tel: +81-45-641-1496

Once Japan was opened up the rest of the world, Yokohama rapidly developed a thriving silk trade and Indian merchants were quick to settle in the port town. Among the many Indian restaurants in the City today, Sitar is very popular for its interesting selection of North

Indian dishes prepared by invited Indian chefs.

SuraBaya *(Indonesian)*
Shinminatocho 11 Banchi, Naka-ku, Yokohama City,
Kanagawa Prefecture 231-0001 Japan
Tel: +81-45-222-2577

The rather Balinese atmosphere is a surprise on the
5th floor of the World Porters complex at Yokohama's
portside. The food is authentically Indonesian and the
staff warm and friendly.

Okinawa Tei   *(Japanese)*
3-74-14 Nakadori, Tsurumi-ku, Yokohama City,
Kanagawa Prefecture 230-0042
Tel: +81-45-506-4774

What started out as a shop supplying Okinawan produce
is now a favourite dining spot. Small and informal, it
serves a variety of healthy dishes special to Okinawa.
Ideal if your business trip doesn't permit you to get to
the island of Okinawa itself.

Wakana   *(Japanese)*
5-20 Minatocho, Naka-ku, Yokohama City, Kanagawa
Prefecture 231-0017
Tel: +81-45-681-1404

This favourite Yokohama restaurant has been in business
for something like 130 years. The speciality of the house
is broiled eel and if you have never tried it before, this is
a great place to have your first taste. The menu also has
various fish and chicken dishes on offer but the eel is
without a doubt worth a visit as is the traditional
atmosphere and the grace of the kimono-clad waitresses.

Other places

Tokyo is not Japan, just as London is not Britain, Paris
not France and so on. If you have the chance to travel
outside of the capital city you will understand much
more about what makes Japan such an extraordinary
country. This handbook has focused on just a few
places that might be of interest. There are, of course,
many more.

Chukagui
Odori

Ichiba Dori

Kanagawa-ken Dori

10

leisure and tourism

leisure and tourism

Things to do and see in Japan

You've had your meetings, the trade mission has gone well and suddenly you find yourself with a little time that you can call your own. What do you do? Depending on just how much time you have, Japan has a great deal to offer. Here are a few suggestions.

Looping the loop

If all you have is a morning or an afternoon and you're not up to anything very strenuous, an interesting way to get a sense of Tokyo as a city is to ride the entire loop of the Yamanote Line. It circles the city and all but two of its 29 stations have connections with other subway lines or suburban railway lines. Since it connects all of Tokyo's major sub-centres, you will quickly understand that while the city may look like one huge urban sprawl, it is actually a conglomeration of smaller communities that differ greatly, from what is known as *shita-machi* (translated as down town but actually meaning the old centre of town) to the modern centres of business and commerce. Ideally you will choose to get off here and there to sample some of the locales, but even staying on the train is a worthwhile (and inexpensive) small adventure: station by station the make up of the passengers changes: the trendy young, the serious businessman, the farmers – often elderly woman with large baskets on their backs – coming into town to sell their produce. But a word of warning: avoid the rush hours. The Yamanote Line is one of Tokyo's busiest and although the train runs are as frequent as every two or three minutes at certain times of day, they can be extremely – and uncomfortably – crowded.

If you are going to consider this option (or indeed any that involves significant city travel) it is well worth buying one of the pre-paid travel cards such as PASMO or SUICA. They are available in denominations from ¥1,000 to ¥10,000 and they allow you to pass through the automatic gates without having to buy a ticket. Such cards may also be used on the city's buses and, increasingly they may be used to buy small items such as soft drinks or snacks from vending machines or station kiosks.

10

Sky high

Another way to take in all of Tokyo – and Yokohama, too, for that matter – is to see it from the air. **Excel Air Service** (http://www.excel-air.com/english/index.html) offers a variety of what it calls "helicopter cruises" which are remarkably reasonable in price and which allow you 15-20 minutes circling above the city's outstanding landmarks.

Cultural bites

A good way to spend an hour or so getting a real taste of traditional Japanese culture is to visit the Kabuki-za, a splendid theatre in the Ginza. The three Chinese characters that make up the name *Ka-bu-ki* literally translate as song, dance and skill and certainly these productions deliver plenty of all three. Kabuki is one of the three classical Japanese theatrical forms, along with the somewhat less accessible *No* and *Bunraku*. It is performed only by male actors and then only by those who are themselves the sons of *kabuki* actors (it is not unusual for people to be adopted into a theatrical family to ensure the continuation of the lineage). The actors who play the female roles (*onnagata*) attract particular attention for the way they capture feminine grace and beauty without appearing in the least effeminate: this is no drag act! Some, such as Tamasaburo Bando, enjoy star status and have large followings of fans. Some have taken their talents beyond the *kabuki* stage and into mainstream theatre, playing to great acclaim in Bando's case Queen Elizabeth I.

The plots of *kabuki* plays are filled with romance, bravery, self-sacrifice (including, often suicide) and the stories are told in song and dynamic dances on elaborate sets and against colourful backdrops. The make-up is highly stylized – as is the manner of speaking the dialogue – and the costumes are lavish and subject to astonishingly quick changes; the wings of a *kabuki* theatre are like a pit stop at a race track, with the quick change so finely choreographed that an entire costume of several layers can be changed in a matter of a few seconds. One frequently performed play that demonstrates this to superb effect is the five-act *Yoshitsune sembon-zakura* (Yoshitsune's thousand cherry trees) in which one of the

10

characters is a fox that can take on human form
(a common theme in traditional Japanese stories).
First seen in 1747, this is one of the three most often
produced plays in the *kabuki* canon and is an excellent
introduction to the form.

Such dramas can take several hours to play out, but it is
possible to buy tickets for just one act; enough to get a
taste of the sheer spectacle that is *kabuki* and to take in
the unique atmosphere in the playhouse. Most hotels
should be able to arrange tickets and to advise on which
act is most likely to please. Once at the theatre you can
rent a headset that will allow you to hear a synchronised
English-language explanation of the story you are watching.

A taste of the past

Tokyo is a city rich in culture and there are literally
hundreds of museums, some of which specialize in such
things as paper, *sake* (Japanese rice-wine) and *samurai*
swords in addition to the obvious classical collections.

One favourite among foreign visitors is the **Fukugawa
Edo Museum** at Monzen-Nakacho on the Tozai Subway
Line. What makes it special is that it is a recreation of a
part of Edo (the city that became known as Tokyo) so
that visitors can get a sense of what life was like around
the 17th century. The reconstruction is life-size and it is
possible to enter buildings such as shops selling rice and
vegetables and to wander around the narrow streets.
The museum also has a canal.

A more traditional museum that deals with the same
subject is the Edo-Tokyo Museum at Ryogoku on the
JR Sobu Line or Oedo Subway Line (the area is most
famous for being the home of Sumo). The museum
covers almost 30,000 square metres and houses a
permanent exhibition of relics and replicas as well as
special exhibitions that change fairly frequently. There
are volunteer bi-lingual guides to help you make the
most of a visit.

A goddess of mercy and a driverless train

Let's say you have a whole day to spare. You can divide
your time between the ancient and the modern. A visit to

10

Asakusa will introduce you shita-machi. The main focus of your visit will be a Buddhist temple known as Sensoji. It is also known as the Asakusa Kannon Temple, after the Buddhist goddess of mercy of that name, whose statue was dredged from the nearby Sumida River. Built in 645, this is the city's oldest temple and is truly a Japan icon. The approach to the temple is through the Kaminarimon (Thunder Gate) on either side of which is a fierce-looking protective deity and over which hangs a famously enormous red lantern. The street leading to the second gate (Hozomon) is called the Nakamise and it is lined with small shops dealing in everything from snacks to woodblock prints, from fans to kimono. This is a good place to pick up interesting souvenirs at reasonable prices.

Once behind the second gate, the temple grounds open up into quite a large area with the main temple building ahead and a five-storey-ed red pagoda to the left. Such pagodas (usually with three or five storeys) normally hold a relic of the Buddha – perhaps a tooth or some of his hair, normally of course in representation. Nearby there is also the Asakusa Shrine which was built in 1649 by Tokugawa Ieyasu and which, annually beginning on the third Friday in May, holds the three-day Sanja Festival – one of the country's most famous – and certainly worth considering if your visit should happen to coincide with it.

Before approaching the temple steps and making a small offering, it is customary to "cleanse" oneself in the incense smoke: a large receptacle right in front of the building gives off a constant cloud of the pungent smoke that you can pat into your hair and over your clothes. You can of course buy your own incense to ensure it remains constant! (The ritual before entering a shrine on the other hand is to wash your hands in water and rinse your mouth using a conveniently provided ladle with a bamboo handle.) Also in the area are temple stalls selling votive tablets and an assortment of amulets that promise to keep away evil, ensure safe travel, success in exams or an easy childbirth: you name it, there seems to be an amulet designed to handle it. Sales of these items go toward the maintenance of the temple and its grounds which is a very short walk from Asakusa Station on the Ginza and Asakusa subway lines. If you are tempted to explore the area beyond the temple itself you can take a ride in a jinriksha – a small carriage that's pulled along (surprisingly quickly) by some very strong "drivers" most of whom are dressed in Edo-style uniforms.

The temple is also very close to the **Sumida River** – one of Japan's largest and most important. From the pier close by the subway station you can take a variety of cruises down the river, allowing for a very different perspective of the city. Taking one such cruise to the area known as **Odaiba**, will allow you to see something of present-day Tokyo, both in terms at looking back over the astonishing city skyline but also in what's available at Odaiba itself, a late 1990s waterfront project built on reclaimed land that features futuristic architecture (for example the striking Fuji Television Building) and a variety of shopping malls, restaurants and other entertainments. It is very popular with young people and a popular dating spot in the evening when the view back across to the brightly lit city is nothing less than spectacular.

To get back to the city, take the **Yurikamome** to Shimbashi station. This fully automated transit system runs on rubber wheels on an elevated concrete track and has no driver or guard on board. Everything is controlled by computers. A highlight of the trip back into town is that the Yurikamome crosses the **Rainbow Bridge**, a span of some 570 metres (1870 ft) affording unrivalled views of Tokyo Bay on one side and the Tokyo Tower area of the capital on the other. Arriving at Shimbashi, you are a short walk away from the **Ginza**, Japan's most famous shopping and entertainment areas and the most expensive real estate in the whole of Japan. The Shimbashi area also has a large number of restaurants ranging from the cheap-and-cheerful to the very expensive. (The deservedly Michelin-starred Sushi JIRO is in this location.)

Should you wish to spend some time in the Ginza, there are a number of department stores, the most famous of which is Wako, sometimes referred to as the Harrods of Tokyo because of its emphasis on selling luxury goods. A short walk away is Kyukyudo, a shop that specialises in incense, Japanese paper (*washi*), a surprisingly large variety of items made of that paper and the inks and brushes used in traditional Japanese calligraphy (*shodo*).

10

This is definitely worth a visit and is a good source of small gifts with a genuinely Japanese flavour. Finally, if your expense account permits it, you might want to end your day with a meal at BEIGE, a restaurant that is a joint venture between Chanel and celebrated chef Alain Ducasse and which is appropriately located atop the Chanel building in the Ginza. Dinner options start from ¥17,000 (€110.00, $160.00) without wine, tax and service.

Iris Gardens and an electric town

Another combination of ancient and modern (that could also include some exciting shopping opportunities) starts at Omotesando station (Chiyoda, Ginza, and Hanzomon subway lines) and a walk down the street that has been dubbed the Champs-Élysée of Tokyo. It is easy to see why. **Omotsesando Dori** is wider than most Japanese city streets, it is lined on both sides by Zelkova trees and the area is home to many of the big international fashion houses. It is closed off to traffic on Sundays to become a "pedestrian paradise" and is very popular with the young and fashionable (especially those with serious money to spend). On the right as you walk down the street towards Harajuku there is the **Omotesando Hills** complex of shops, boutiques and restaurants. This is a project of the Mori Building Group which was also responsible for the **Roppongi Hills** "city within a city" including the 54 storey Mori Tower and the Grand Hyatt Hotel. The Group's President, Minoru Mori, has a striking vision: he wants nothing other than to change the face of Tokyo completely and in doing so, to change the way in which Tokoites live. Already he has published plans for a further development that will match – if not exceed – the scale of Roppongi Hills. This is itself well worth a visit, if only to go to the observation deck and take advantage of a 360 degree panorama of Tokyo and its surroundings; it is – for now – a unique chance to really grasp the size and spread of this exciting city and if the weather conditions are right you'll have a spectacular view of Mount Fuji.

Further down Omotesando Dori and on the left, you will find the **Oriental Bazaar**, a very popular place with foreign travellers looking for souvenirs that will allow them to take back to their own countries a true taste of Japan. Recently refurbished, there are several floors of merchandise ranging from scenic postcards and inexpensive trinkets to far more expensive orginal woodblock prints by such masters as Hokkusai and items of antique furniture such as traditional Japanese chests (*tansu*). There is, of course, much in between such as traditional pottery or lacquer ware and well-executed reproductions of old Japanese prints that are much more affordable than the originals.

The avenue ends at **Harajuku**, long a favourite of the city's youth culture where Takeshita Street is very much a reminder of London's Carnaby Street in its hey day. More affordable at this end of the avenue, the fashion ranges from Gothic to Rockabilly, from Hip Hop to Punk and the up-market cafés give way to fast food outlets and stalls selling crêpes and exotic ice-creams (think sweet potato, black sesame and pumpkin to name just three of many).

In stark contrast to this, a matter of a few minutes away an oasis of extreme calm awaits. Right by Harajuku Station (Yamanote Line) is the **Meiji Jingu Shrine**. Dating from 1920, this is where the Emperor Meiji and his consort Empress Shoken are enshrined. In fact the original buildings were destroyed during the second world war air raids and what we see today are 1958 reconstructions. The 700,000 square metre site is actually a forest of some 120,000 evergreen trees of more than 350 varieties. They were originally donated by people from all over Japan as a sign of respect for the Emperor who opened up their country and set it on the course of modernisation. The long walk from the Harajuku entrance to the main building is itself a kind of meditation when the stillness of the forest makes it difficult to believe that you are actually in the heart of one of the most hectic cities in the world. The site was chosen because it is centred on an iris garden that the Emperor and Empress often visited. The garden still exists and in season (late June – early July) is visited by thousands of Japanese from all over the country anxious to take in the beauty of millions of irises and capture it on camera. Most foreign visitors to the Shrine find it a rewarding experience and should your trip to Japan coincide with the iris season, that will be an added bonus.

10

On your return to Harajuku station you have a chance to take in the still futuristic-looking buildings that architect Kenzo Tange created for the 1964 Olympics and behind them the tower of the NHK broadcasting centre before taking the Yamanote Line from Harajuku station to **Akihabara**.

The name Akihabara translates as "field of autumn leaves" but nothing could be further from a true description of this area of Tokyo that is affectionately known as Electric Town. This sobriquet stems from the district's emergence during the 80s and 90s as *the* place to go to buy the latest electronic appliances at the best possible prices. In fact it was (and still is) possible to buy everything from the smallest electronics components needed by those building their own ham radios to the most sophisticated sound systems not to mention such domestic applicances as refrigerators, washing machines, air conditioners and so on. In the 90s the area soon developed a reputation for also having the best deals on personal computers and software products. The major outlets such as Laox, BIC Camera and others – many of which offer tax-free sales for visitors – sit cheek-by-jowl along the main thoroughfare making competition very intense; this is perhaps the only part of town in which you can even think of bartering over the price of items.

However, times have changed. People don't buy CD players, let alone Hi-Fi systems like they used to and many of the same vendors have opened discount outlets in other parts of town (for example Shinjuku, Shibuya, and Ikebukuro). So while Akihabara is still a good place to look for bargains in its traditionally strong areas (especially tax-free), it is also worth a visit for what it has more recently become: a mecca for the *otaku* crowd. *Otaku* is a term that is used to describe someone with an obsessive interest in something, usually video games, *manga* (comic books) and *anime* (animation). This obsession has also given rise to a phenomenon known as cosplay (a contraction of costume play) where people dress up as any one of a number of characters from their favourite comics, animated movies or video games, sometimes to enact specific scenes and sometimes to improvise others. They do this largely for themselves rather than as performance art *per se*, but it can make for entertaining street theatre especially as many of the costumes are extremely eleborate with great attention paid to the minutest details. Akihabara (along with Harajuku) is a favourite gathering spot and there are a number of cosplay cafés in the area. The waitresses sport a variety of costumes, the most popular of which appears to be that of a Victorian parlourmaid, hence the nickname meido café.

Around town

If you don't feel quite up to manouevering the city's public transport system (not nearly as daunting as you might think, and local people are almost universally helpful) you can opt for one of the many organised half-day or whole-day tours by luxury sight-seeing coach. These are generally organised into guided tours that take in the traditional sights such as shrines and gardens, those that focus on modern-day Tokyo, and those which offer a "cultural experience" such as the Japanese tea ceremony (*chado*) or flower arrangement (*ikebana*). Some tours combine all these elements. Most of the major hotels can make arrangements for you to join a tour and they normally have brochures galore to help you make your choice. If you are lucky the tour may actually start and finish at your hotel or at least the coach might call at it en route. However, if you want to get an idea of just what is available and what the experience might be like – as well as how much it will cost you – you can visit http://www.hatobus.com/en/index.html, the site of Hato Bus, one of the most popular providers of such tours. It is by no means the only company doing so but it does enjoy a fine reputation for good organisation and the professionalism of its bilingual guides.

10

Out of town

To see Tokyo is not necessarily to see Japan. Fortunately it is possible to get out of town, even for just one day. Many of the same companies that operate the Tokyo tours offer a variety of packages that take in other areas such as Mt Fuji and the five lakes at Hakone, as well as the venues suggested below. But armed with the appropriate map, often freely available at hotels or train stations, it is possible to make your own itinerary.

Kamakura

This former centre of political power (see Chapter One)
is a coastal town to the south of Tokyo and less than
an hour from Tokyo Station by the JR Yokosuka Line.
JR offers what it calls the "Kamakura Enoshima Free
Kippu" which includes the Tokyo-Kamakura round
trip and unlimited free travel by train and bus in the
Kamakura area and at under ¥2,000 is a bargain.

Kamakura is popular with both foreign and Japanese
visitors because of its many temples and shrines. There
are a number of hiking routes that allow you to take
in a number of these sites and free bi-lingual maps are
available at both Kamakura and Kitakamakura Stations,
the starting points for most of these hikes.

Taking the Enoden Streetcar three short stops from
Kamakura (included in the Free Kippu) you will arrive
at Hase Station and the site of the most visited Kamakura
icon, the *Daibutsu* or Great Buddha. At Thirteeen and a
half metres tall – the second largest such figure in Japan
– the bronze Amida Buddha is in the grounds of the
Kotokuin Temple. It dates back to 1252 and was
originally housed in wooden buildings. These, however,
were washed away in a great tsunami in the late 15th
century and the statue has remained exposed to the
elements ever since.

A short walk from the Daibutsu is *Hasedera* (Hase
Temple) most famous for its 9.18 metre tall gilded figure
of Kannon, the Goddess of Mercy. This eleven-headed
statue is the largest such wooden figure in Japan and is
impressively housed in the main temple building which
itself sits in magnificent grounds complete with a cave
containing numerous images of Benten, a goddess of
feminine beauty and wealth, ponds, a variety of trees
and shrubs and literally thousands of hydrangeas
which, in season (June – July), are spectacular. The
Homotsu-kan Museum in the temple grounds houses a
variety of important national cultural properties as well
as archeological items that were discovered during the
1992 reconstruction of the site. From the observation
deck just outside the main building there is a stunning
view across the city of Kamakura and the Shonan

10

beaches, the black volcanic sandy lure for Japan's young surfers who flock here in droves.

A ten minute walk from Kamakura Station is the most important of the area's Shinto Shrines. **Tsurugaoka Hachimangu** was founded in 1063 and moved to its current site in 1180 by the first Shogun of the Kamakura Government. The nearby park is famous for the lotuses that flourish in its ponds and in April and September the broad lane approaching the Shrine is the venue for impressive displays of *yabusame* (archery on horseback).

If your day allows you time for a little souvenir hunting, you might consider some of the lacquer ware for which Kamakura is famous. Zen Buddhism was introduced to Japan from China during the Kamakura Period and along with it came various arts and crafts. The technique of lacquer was among these and although many other areas of Japan also produce lacquer goods, those produced in Kamakura have a very distinct character, both in terms of the carvings that are used and the final colour of the products.

Nikko

Another possible one-day trip is to the **Nikko National Park**, 125 kilometers north of Tokyo and a little under two hours by the Tobu Line from Asakusa to Nikko Station. Once again it is possible to buy a "free pass" that covers the basic round trip and unlimited local travel.

The City of Nikko is best known for being the home of the **Toshogu Shrine**, the mausoleum of Tokugawa Ieyasu. It is striking for its lavish decoration – Shinto Shrines are generally very subdued and simple – with the use of a great deal of gold leaf and ornate wooden carvings. One of the most famous of these is the three wise monkeys who see no evil, speak no evil, and hear no evil. In fact the complex is a collection of around a dozen Shinto and Buddhist buildings set in a beautiful forest known to be home to numerous wild – if not necessarily wise – monkeys.

A short and spectacular bus ride from the centre of Nikko City will take you to *Chuzenji-ko* (Lake

10

Chuzenji). The ride is spectacular because it takes you 400 metres up the so-called *Irohazaka*, a winding road that consists of some 48 needlepoint turns (in fact, there are two separate roads; one going up, the other down). The lake itself sits at the foot of a volcano, Mount Nantai, and is surrounded by forest. In the autumn (October-November) these present themselves in a magnificent tapestry of crimsons and oranges, yellows and golds, as the leaves of the maples, zelkovas and other trees change colour. The Japanese call this *koyo* and the ritual viewing of them is as important as viewing the cherry blossoms in spring. Chuzenji is also known for its waterfalls, in particular the 97- meter high *Kegon-no-Take* (Kegon Falls) and the *Ryuzu-no-Take* (Dragon's Head Falls) that stretch for over 210 metres.

Close by the Kegon Falls is the *Chuzuji Onsen*, a hot spring resort. *Onsen* (hot spring baths in which the water contains a variety of minerals and other elements considered to be good for the body and mind) are popular all over Japan and soaking in one for a while is a tremendous way to relax and is highly recommended. Just to be careful to follow the rules of bathhouse courtesy: before entering the bath itself, use the shower area to thoroughly soap, shampoo and scrub and only when you're completely rinsed of any soap, immerse yourself in the hot spring. Carefully: when they say hot spring, they mean hot!

Further afield

If you are in the very fortunate position of having more than one free day and can consider an overnight (or two-night) stay, you might want to consider taking the bullet train[3] to another ancient capital, *Kyoto*.

The "western capital" was mercifully spared the fire-bombing of the Second World War and is thus one of best preserved of Japan's historic centres. Japan's capital for more than ten centuries, it remains home today to

---

[3] Be sure to order your Japan Rail Pass before you leave home; you will save considerably. But be aware, too, that on certain train runs – for example the very fastest Nozomi – you cannot use the Pass. Full details are at http://www.japanrailpass.net/eng/en001.html

10

thousands of shrines and temples and areas such as Gion – the exclusive *geisha* district – that appear to have changed little in centuries.

Kyoto is famous also for its cuisine, in particular the vegetarian dishes favoured by monks. For a truly Japanese experience stay in a *Kyoto ryokan* (Japanese style inn). You will sleep in futon on *tatami* mats, eat exquisitely prepared food designed to satisfy the eye as much as the appetite and soak in a hot spring bath (if you are lucky it may be a *rotenburo* – an open air bath).

There is so much in Kyoto that is worth visiting that it is hard to know where to begin: perhaps Kiyomizudera ("Pure Water") Temple, which is famous for its large wooden terrace built on the hill side in eastern Kyoto. Dating back to 780 it is a UNESCO world heritage site – one of 17 in the area. The spring water that gives the temple its name is said to have healing properties.

Nearby is *Sanjusangendo* ("Hall of the Lotus King") which is famous for its 1001 statues of Kannon the goddess of mercy. The temple was founded in 1164 and the main hall, which houses the statues, is Japan's longest wooden structure – it's over 100 metres long. In its centre there is one large Kannon and that is flanked on either side by 500 smaller statues each as tall as a human being.

10

Other famous sites are the *Kinkakuji* (Golden) Pavilion which is covered in gold leaf and the *Ginkakuji* (Silver) Pavilion which, though beautiful, is not actually silver at all. The *Ryoanji* Temple, meanwhile, is best known for its rock garden. The "Temple of the Peaceful Dragon" is one of Zen Buddhism's most iconic.

If you only have one whole day to spare in Kyoto it probably makes sense to sign up for one of the guided tours that your hotel can arrange for you. Indeed if you know in advance that you will have such free time, your travel agent at home can make the arrangements before you leave for Japan. If, on the other hand, you have the luxury of two or three days, you might want to choose your own itinerary.

You might choose to include a visit to *Nara*, Japan's first permanent capital and less than an hour by train from Kyoto. Many of the ancient city's main attractions are located in or around the Nara Park which is home to hundreds of freely roaming deer, believed in Shinto (the indigenous faith of the Japanese) to be messengers of the gods.

One such attraction is *Todaiji* ("Great Eastern Temple") the world's largest wooden building housing Japan's largest Buddha image. Parts of the *Horyuji Temple* on the other hand are the world's oldest surviving wooden structures. This "Temple of the Flourishing Law" was founded by Prince Shotoku who is credited with introducing Buddhism to Japan (see Chapter One).

Another option that is further away from Tokyo (but still easily accessed by bullet train) is *Hiroshima*, the city that was destroyed in the first ever use of nuclear weapons over a populated area. A visit to the *Peace Memorial Park* is sobering to say the least and most people, whatever their views on the use of nuclear weapons, find it deeply moving. The *Atomic Bomb Dome* is one of the few buildings around the explosion's epicenter that partially survived the blast. A short train and ferry ride from the City of Hiroshima is *Miyajima* – literally "shrine island". Considered one of Japan's three most scenic views, it is certainly one of the most recognizable. It is most famous for the *Itsukushima Shrine* and a striking large red wooden torii (gate) that at high tide appears to rise up out of the ocean.

It is not possible in one short chapter to do more than offer a few suggestions for possible excursions. But if your trip to Japan allows, getting out of Tokyo is strongly to be recommended. A very useful resource (and one often gratefully consulted in the preparation of this chapter) is the website http://www.japan-guide.com. You might also want to visit another very resource-rich and attractive site http://www.jnto.go.jp/ belonging to the Japan National Tourist Organisation. Bon voyage!

appendix one   A1

appendix one

Airlines

The following international airlines have representation in Japan:

(047 numbers are Narita airport desks. 03 numbers are the Tokyo offices. 0120 numbers are toll-free customer services centres.)

Airline	Telephone
Aeroflot	Tel: 047-634-3944 Tel: 03-5532-8701
Air Canada	Tel: 03-5405-8800
Air China	Tel: 03-5251-0711
Air France	Tel: 047-632-7710 Tel: 03-3570-8577
Air India	Tel: 047-634-8261 Tel: 03-3508-0261
Air Japan	Tel: 0120-029-120
Air New Zealand	Tel: 047-634-8388 Tel: 0120-300-747
Air Niugini	Tel: 03-5216-3555
Air Pacific	Tel: 03-5208-5171
Air Tahiti Nui	Tel: 047-632-7710 Tel: 03-6267-1177
Aircalin (c/o Air France)	Tel: 03-3570-8755
Alitalia	Tel: 047-632-7811
All Nippon Airways	Tel: 0120-029-333
American Airlines	Tel: 03-4550-2111
Asiana	Tel: 03-5812-6600
Austrian Airlines	Tel: 047-634-8411 Tel: 03-5222-5454
British Airways	Tel: 0120-122-881 Tel:03-3570-8657
Cathay Pacific	Tel: 047-632-7650 Tel: 03-5159-1700
China Airlines	Tel: 03-5520-0333

A1

A1

China Eastern Airlines	Tel: 047-634-3945
	Tel: 03-3506-1166
China Southern Airlines	Tel: 03-5157-8011
Continental Airlines	Tel: 03-5464-5050
	Tel: 0120-24-2414
Continental Micronesia	Tel: 03-5464-5050
Delta Airlines	Tel: 03-3593-6666
	Tel: 0120-333-742
Egyptair	Tel: 047-634-8391
	Tel: 03-3211-4521
Eva Air	Tel: 03-5798-2811
Finnair	Tel: 047-632-7600
	Tel: 0120-700-915
Garuda Indonesia	Tel: 047-634-8377
	Tel: 03-3240-6161
IBEX Air	Tel: 03-6741-6688
	Tel: 0120-029-222
Iran Air	Tel: 047-634-8372
	Tel: 03-3586-2101
Japan Airlines	Tel: 0120-255-931
	Tel: 03-5460-0533
J-Air	Tel: 0120-255-971
KLM	Tel: 047-632-5720
	Tel: 03-3570-8770
Korean Air	Tel: 047-632-7561
	Tel: 03-5443-3311
Lufthansa	Tel: 047-634-8130
	Tel: 03-4333-7656
	Tel: 0120-051-844
Malayasia Airlines	Tel: 047-634-8270
	Tel: 03-5733-2111
Miat Mongolian Airlines	Tel: 03-5615-4653
Northwest Airlines	Tel: 047-632-7411
	Tel: 0120-120-747
Pakistan International	Tel: 03-3216-6511

Philippine Airlines	Tel: 047-634-8381
	Tel: 03-5157-4362
Qantas	Tel: 047-634-8285
	Tel: 03-3593-7000
SAS	Tel: 047-634-8415
	Tel: 03-5400-2331
Singapore Airlines	Tel: 047-632-7591
	Tel: 03-3213-3431
SriLankan Airlines	Tel: 03-3431-6600
Swiss	Tel: 047-634-8320
	Tel: 012-667-788
Thai Airways	Tel: 047-634-8329
	Tel: 0570-064-015
THY Turkish Airlines	Tel: 047-634-8310
United Airlines	Tel: 03-3817-4411
	Tel: 0120-114-466
US Airways	Tel: 03-3597-9471
Uzbekistan Airways	Tel: 03-5157-0722
Vietnam Airlines	Tel: 03-3508-1481
Virgin Atlantic	Tel: 03-3499-8811

A1

Airports

(See also Chapter Three)

Japan's main international airports are in Tokyo, Osaka, Nagoya and Fukuoka

Tokyo

Narita International   Information: 0476-34-8000
                            Website: www.narita-airport.jp

Tokyo

Haneda   Information: 03-5757-8111
                   Website: www.tokyo-airport-bldg.co.jp/en/

Osaka

Kansai International Airport

                            Information: 072-455-2500
                     Website: www.kansai-airport.or.jp/en/

Nagoya

Central Japan International Airport

Information: 0569-38-1195

Website: www.centrair.jp/en/

Fukuoka

Fukuoka International Airport

Information: 092-621-6059 (Domestic)

092-621-0303 (International)

Website: www.fuk-ab.co.jp

Banking/Credit cards

(See also Chapter Four)

Japan's high street banks are open from 09.00 to 15.00 Monday through Friday except for Japanese National Holidays. ATMs operate outside of these times and some so-called "convenience stores" such as 7-11, Sankus, Lawsons etc., have ATMs that theoretically operate 24 hours a day. However, it is unwise to assume that your usual cash card will work in Japan; some do and some don't and, unfortunately, there's no authoritative listing of which is which. Many a business traveller has been caught short of cash and with no immediately obvious means of obtaining any. Foreign banks in general do not have retail operations in Japan. The exceptions are Citibank and HSBC but neither has branch networks that extend much outside of the major cities.

Major credit cards are much more broadly accepted than they used to be even a few years ago but Japan is still essentially a cash-based society and if you expect to be travelling outside of the major urban centres, it is better to play safe and have a good supply of cash with you. The good news is that Japan is still a relatively crime-free country so carrying large amounts of cash is much less stressful that it might be in some other world capitals.

At the time of writing there is an increasing interest in pre-paid cards that can be used to pay for buses, subways, trains, taxis and other small purchases ("Suica" and "Pasmo" for example) and some suppliers make it possible to use a cell phone as a pre-paid card.

A1

Business support services
General support

The Japan External Trade Organisation (JETRO)
has Business Support Centres in Tokyo, Yokohama,
Nagoya, Osaka, Kobe and Fukuoka. Their aim is to
provide one-stop support and service to foreign firms
seeking to set-up business in Japan. With access to the
relevant government ministries and agencies, the centres
provide free temporary office space, consultations with
expert advisors and access to a wealth of business
information. The Tokyo and Osaka centres have
particularly extensive libraries of reference materials.

JETRO has offices in major cities around the world and
it can be a useful exercise to see what advice they might
offer before setting out on a business trip, especially if
it is a first-time visit. The organisation's website is at
www.jetro.go.jp/

Interpreters and translators

Most of the international hotels in Japan's main cities
have business centres which can help with arranging
such things as interpreters and translators. But an
internet search will show that there are literally
thousands of
such services available commercially. Among them are:

AIT Language Services Website: www.aitkk.com/

Japan Convention Services Website: www.jcs-pco.com/

Simul International
Website: www.simul.co.jp/en/top.html

Translators Café
Website: www.translatorscafe.com/cafe/default.asp

Temporary office space

A number of companies offer short-term temporary
office space and sometimes even virtual office services.
Among them are:

Regus Website: www.regus.com

Servcorp Website: www.servcorp.net

A1

Chambers of commerce & business groups

Foreign business in Japan is well served by a network of strong chambers of commerce and business groups, many of which take part in regular joint activities such as the twice yearly survey of business confidence. Visitors are often welcome to attend chamber functions. A visit to a chamber's website will let you know what activities are taking place during your time in Japan and it is then simply a matter of an e-mail or a 'phone call to confirm that you can take part.

Name of Chamber   **Contact details**

American Chamber of Commerce in Japan
Tel: 03-3433-5381   Fax: 03-3433-8454
Email: info@accj.or.jp   Website: www.accj.or.jp

Arab Business Group
Tel: 03-6222-0888   Fax: 03-6222-0855
                    Email: many.sultan@aas-associates.com

Australian & New Zealand Chamber of Commerce
in Japan
Tel: 03-5312-1988   Fax: 03-5312-1989
Email: exec.director@anzccj.jp   Website: www.anzccj.jp

Austrian Business Council   Tel: 03-3403-1777
Fax: 03-3403-3407   Email: tokio@austratrade-jp.org

Belgian-Luxembourg Chamber of Commerce in Japan
Tel: 03-5761-8071   Fax: 03-5761-8072
Email: info@blccj.or.jp   Website: www.blccj.or.jp

Brazilian Chamber of Commerce in Japan
Tel: 03-3597-5310   Fax: 3597-5311
Email: management@ccbj.jp   Website: www.ccbj.jp

British Chamber of Commerce in Japan
Tel: 03-3267-1901   Fax: 03-3267-1903
Email: info@bccjapan.com Website: www.bccjapan.com

Canadian Chamber of Commerce in Japan
Tel: 03-5775-9500   Fax: 03-57759507
Email: info@cccj.or.jp   Website: www.cccj.or.jp

A1

Danish Chamber of Commerce in Japan
Tel: 03-3780-8729   Fax: 03-3476-4234
Email: dccj@um.dk   Website: www.denmark.or.jp

European Business Council
(*the trade policy arm of the European national*
chambers)
Tel: 03-3263-6222   Fax: 03-3263-6223
Email: ebc@gol.com   Website: www.ebc-jp.com

Finnish Chamber of Commerce in Japan
Tel: 03-5450-7207   Fax: 03-5450-7208
Email: fccj@gol.com   Website: www.fcc.or.jp

French Chamber of Commerce & Industry in Japan
Tel: 03-3288-9621   Fax: 03-3288-9558
Email: info@ccifj.or.jp   Website: www.ccifj.or.jp

German Chamber of Commerce & Industry in Japan
Tel: 03-5276-9811   Fax: 03-5276-8733
Email: info@dihkj.or.jp   Website: www.japan.ahk.de

Indian Community Activities   Tel: 03-3727-4417
Fax:03-3727-4419   Email: manicat@gol.com
Website: www.manicat.org

Ireland Japan Chamber of Commerce
Tel: 03-3263-0695   Fax: 03-3265-2265
Email: secretariat @ijcc.jp   Website: www.ijcc.jp

Italian Chamber of Commerce in Japan
Tel: 03-3560-1100   Fax: 03-3560-1105
Email: iccj@iccj.or.jp   Website: www.iccj.or.jp

Netherlands Chamber of Commerce in Japan
Tel: 044-246-1355   Fax: 044-246-1355
Email: nccj@nccj.jp   Website: www.nccj.jp

Norwegian Chamber of Commerce in Japan
Tel: 03-5475-2611   Fax: 03-3440-2719
Email: stein.saugnes@nccj.or.jp
                                    Website: www.nccj.or.jp

A1

Russian Federation Chamber of Commerce & Industry in Japan
Tel: 03- 3447-3281   Fax: 03-3447-3221

Slovenia Business Group in Japan
Tel: 03-3952-7382   Fax: 03-5996-2076
Email: sethna@hpo.net

Swedish Chamber of Commerce & Industry in Japan
Tel: 03-5211-2101   Fax: 03-5211-2102
Email: sccj@twics.com   Website: www.sccj.org

Swiss Chamber of Commerce & Industry in Japan
Tel: 03-5408-7569   Fax: 03-3433-6066
Email: sccj@gol.com   Website: www.sccij.org

Turkish Chamber of Commerce & Industry in Japan
Tel: 03-5414-2718   Fax: 03-5414-2719
Email: info@tccij.com   Website: www.tccij.com

Currency

Japan's currency is the yen. There are coins valued at one, five, ten, fifty, one-hundred and five-hundred. As for notes the values are one-thousand, two-thousand, five-thousand and ten-thousand.

A1

Embassies

Afghanistan	Tel: 03-5574-7611
	Website: www.afghanembassyjp.com
Algeria	Tel: 03-3711-2661
Argentina	Tel: 03-5420-7101
	Website: www.embargentina.or.jp
Australia	Tel: 03-5232-4111
	Website: www.australia.or.jp
Austria	Tel: 03-3451-8281
	Website: www.austria.or.jp
Bangladesh	Tel: 03-5704-0216
Belarus	Tel: 03-3448-1623
Belgium	Tel: 03-3262-0191

Bolivia	Tel: 03-3499-5441
Brazil	Tel: 03-3404-5211 Website: www.brasemb.or.jp
Brunei Darussalam	Tel: 03-3447-7997
Bulgaria	Tel: 03-3465-1021
Burkina Faso	Tel: 03-3400-7919
Burundi	Tel: 03-3443-7321
Cambodia	Tel: 03-5412-8521 Website: www.cambodianembassy.jp
Cameroon	Tel: 03-5430-4985
Canada	Tel: 03-5412-6200 Website: www.canadanet.or.jp
Chile	Tel: 03-3452-7561 www.chile.or.jp
China	Tel: 03-3403-3388 Website: www.china-embassy.or.jp
Colombia	Tel: 03-3440-6451 Website: www.colombiaembassy.org
Congo	Tel: 03-5820-1580
Costa Rica	Tel: 03-3486-1812
Cote d'Ivoire	Tel: 03-5454-1401
Croatia	Tel: 03-5469-3014
Cuba	Tel: 03-5570-3182
Czech Republic	Tel: 03-3400-8122 Website: www.czechembassy.org
Denmark	Tel: 03-3496-3001 www.demark.or.jp
Djibouti	Tel: 03-5704-0682
Dominican Republic	Tel: 03-3499-6020
Ecuador	Tel: 03-3499-2800 Website: www.ecuador-embassy.or.jp
Egypt	Tel: 03-3770-8022 Website: www.embassy-avenue.jp

A1

El Salvador	Tel: 03-3499-4461
Ethiopia	Tel: 03-5420-6860
Fiji	Tel: 03-3587-2038
Finland	Tel: 03-5447-6000
	www.finland.or.jp
France	Tel: 03-5798-6000
	Website: www.tokyoembassy.com/france.htm
Gabon	Tel: 03-5430-4925
Germany	Tel: 03-5791-7700
	Website: www.germanembassy-japan.org
Ghana	Tel: 03-5410-8631
	Website: www.ghanaembassy.or.jp
Greece	Tel: 03-3403-0871
Guatemala	Tel: 03-3400-1830
Haiti	Tel: 03-3486-7096
Honduras	Tel: 03-3409-1150
Hungary	Tel: 03-3798-8801
India	Tel: 03-3262-2391
	Website: www.embassy-avenue.jp/india
Indonesia	Tel: 03-3441-4201
Iran	Tel: 03-3446-8011
	Website: www.iranembassyjp.com
Iraq	Tel: 03-5499-3231
Ireland	Tel: 03-3263-0695
	Website: www.embassy-avenue.jp/ireland
Israel	Tel: 03-3264-0911
Italy	Tel: 03-3453-5291
	www.embitaly.jp
Jamaica	Tel: 03-3435-1861
Jordan	Tel: 03-5478-7177
Kenya	Tel: 03-3723-4006
	Website: www.embassy-avenue.jp/kenya
Korea (South)	Tel: 03-3452-7611

A1

Kuwait — Tel: 033-3455-0361
Website: www.kuwait-embassy.or.jp

Laos — Tel: 03-5411-2291

Lebanon — Tel: 03-3580-1227

Liberia — Tel: 03-3707-6925

Libiya — Tel: 03-3477-0701

Lithuania — Tel: 03-3408-5091
Website: www.lithemb.or.jp

Luxembourg — Tel: 03-3265-9621
Website: www.luxembourg,or.jp

Madagascar — Tel: 03-3446-7252

Malawi — Tel: 03-3449-3010
Website: www.malawiembassy.org

Malaysia — Tel: 03-3476-3840

Marshall Islands — Tel: 03-5379-1701

Mauritania — Tel: 03-3449-3810

Mexico — Tel: 03-3581-1131
Website: www.embassy-avenue.jp/mexico

Micronesia — Tel: 03-3585-5456

Mongolia — Tel: 03-3469-2088

Morocco — Tel: 03-5485-7171

Mozambique — Tel: 03-5419-0973

Myanmar — Tel: 03-3441-9291
Website: www.myanmar-embassy-tokyo.net

Nepal — Tel: 03-3705-5558
Website: www.nepal-embassy.org

Netherlands — Tel: 03-5776-5400
Website: www.oranda.or.jp

New Zealand — Tel: 03-3467-2271
Website: www.nzembassy.com

Nicaragua — Tel: 03-3499-0400

Nigeria — Tel: 03-5425-8011

Norway — Tel: 03-3440-2611
Website: www.norway.or.jp

A1

Oman	Tel: 03-3402-0877
Pakistan	Tel: 03-5421-7741
	Website: www.pakistanembassyjapan.com/
Panama	Tel: 03-3499-3741
Papua New Guinea	Tel: 03-3454-7801
Paraguay	Tel: 03-3493-3071
Peru	Tel: 03-3406-4243
Philippines	Tel: 03-5562-1600
Poland	Tel: 03-5794-7020
Portugal	Tel: 03-5212-7322
Qatar	Tel: 03-5475-0611
Romania	Tel: 03-3479-0311
Russian Federation	Tel: 03-3583-4224
	Website: www.embassy-avenue.jp/russia
Rwanda	Tel: 03-5752-4255
Saudi Arabia	Tel: 03-3589-5241
Senegal	Tel: 03-3464-8451
Singapore	Tel: 03-3586-9111
Slovakia	Tel: 03-3451-2200
	Website: www.embassy-avenue.jp/slovakia
Slovenia	Tel: 03-5468-6275
South Africa	Tel: 03-3265-3366
	www.rsatk.com
Spain	Tel: 03-3583-8531
Sri Lanka	Tel: 03-3440-6911
	Website: www.lankaembassy.jp
Sudan	Tel: 03-5729-6170
	Website: www.embassy-avenue.jp/sudan
Sweden	Tel: 03-5562-5050
	Website: www.swedenabroad.com
Switzerland	Tel: 03-5449-8400
	Website: www.eda.admin.ch/tokyo

A1

Syria	Tel: 03-3586-8977
Tanzania	Tel: 03-3425-4531
Thailand	Tel: 03-3447-2247
Tunisia	Tel: 03-3511-6622
Turkey	Tel: 03-3470-5131
Uganda	Tel: 03-3462-7107
Ukraine	Tel: 03-5474-9773
United Arab Emirates	Tel: 03-5489-0804
United Kingdom	Tel: 03-5211-1100 www.uknow.com
United States of America	Tel: 03-3224-5000 Website: www.usembassy.state.gov
Uruguay	Tel: 03-3486-1888
Venezuela	Tel: 03-3409-1501
Vietnam	Tel: 03-3466-3311 Website: www.vietnamembassy.jp
Yemen	Tel: 03-3499-7151
Zambia	Tel: 03-3491-0121
Zimbabwe	Tel: 03-3280-0331

A1

Emergencies

Service	Number
Police (Keisatsu)	110
Ambulance (Kyukyu-sha	119
Fire (Kaji)	
Fire-engine (Shobo-sha)	119
Tokyo English Life Line (TELL)	

Free, anonymous telephone counselling and information
03-5774-0992   Website: www.telljp.com

What to do in the event of an earthquake

Japan is one of the world's most earthquake-prone countries. Fortunately the majority of the 'quakes that occur every year are minor; even then they can be frightening, especially to someone unaccustomed to living in an earthquake zone. Should an earthquake occur while you are in Japan, the most important thing is to try to remain calm. If you are indoors, resist the temptation to run outside while the tremor continues: there may be danger from falling glass or other objects. If it is a strong 'quake, try to take protection from falling objects under a sturdy desk or table or in a doorway. If you are using public transport, in a hotel or major public building, listen for the announcements which will be broadcast in Japanese and English and follow any instructions you are given. If you are outside, beware of falling glass and masonry. NHK radio and television will broadcast bi-lingual information following a seismic event. If you are in a coastal area (and remember much of Japan is close to the sea) listen and look out for tsunami warnings and if you happen to be in the mountains be alert for the possibility of landslides.

Food

With more restaurants than any other capital in the world, Tokyo today has to be the leader when it comes to international cuisine. There are literally thousands of world-class restaurants serving everything from Armenian to Zen dishes and everything in between. As of 2008, some of them have Michelin stars. Japan's other major cities have their fair share of international cuisine too, whether that be French, Italian, Indian or Thai. The country's so-called "family restaurants" offer Japanese versions of western favourites such as curry-rice and hamburgers and there is no shortage of the familiar fast-food outlets such as McDonalds, Pizza Express and Starbucks. Meanwhile, the so-called "convenience stores" offer take-out surprises such as potato and mandarin orange sandwiches and other such inventions.

But Japan's own food culture is rich and varied. Once considered wildly exotic and little known outside of Japan, some elements of the Japanese cuisine have found their way to the world's major cities. But not all of them. Here is a listing of some of the cooking styles the curious business traveller may choose to sample.

Name	What is it?
Fugu	Blow-fish. Only licensed chefs are allowed to serve this as the livers of certain fish contain a deadly poison.
Gyoza	Actually, a Chinese dish but enthusiastically adopted by the Japanese, these are small dumplings stuffed with minced pork and seasonings and fried. They are known in some parts of North America as "pot stickers".
Haru Maki	Spring Rolls – originally Chinese but very popular in Japan. Deep fried pancakes filled with minced pork, sometimes also prawns, bamboo shoots and seasonings.
Kaiseki Ryori	Perhaps this is the pinnacle of Japanese cuisine. The meal consists of many courses, each of them small, but beautifully presented and using strictly seasonal ingredients and tableware, sometimes porcelain, sometimes lacquer. The courses are usually served by women dressed in beautiful kimono who will often explain the significance of the ingredients. This kind of meal can be extremely expensive.
Katsu-don	Slices of deep fried pork fillet with beaten egg, served on top of rice.
Kushi Katsu	Skewers of fish, seafood and vegetables breaded and deep fried.
Nabe	Meat or fish, cooked in one pot together with a variety of vegetables in a rich stock.
Obento	Literally a "boxed lunch". This can be anything from a very inexpensive selection packed in cardboard and bought at a train station (or indeed on the train if it is a Shinkansen) to an extremely expensive kaiseki menu in a lacquer box. Obento are also sold

A1

	in convenience stores and department stores.
Oden	A typical winter dish it consists of a variety of ingredients – boiled eggs, tofu, konyaku, potatoes and more – cooked together in a rich soup.
Okonomiyaki	Typical of Hiroshima and Osaka, this is one of Japan's original fast foods and one that you usually get to make yourself. Various ingredients are combined in a flour-based pancake.
Oshinko	Pickles – there is an almost endless variety of pickled vegetables that are served as a side dish in Japanese meals.
Rāmen	Strictly speaking a Chinese dish, but very popular in Japan. Noodles served in a soup with a variety of added ingredients, usually pork and vegetables.
Robatayaki	Fresh ingredients such as steak, fish, abalone and prawns are grilled in front of the customer and passed to them on a wooden paddle.
Shabu-shabu	Thin slices of beef or pieces of seafood which the customer cooks in a pan of boiling water at the table. The resulting stock is then used to make a soup to which noodles are often added to round out the meal. The name derives from the sound the food makes as it is swished through the water by the chopsticks.
Shumai	Actually Chinese but very popular in Japan, these are steamed dumplings containing either pork or shrimp (sometimes both) and served with a dipping sauce.
Soba	Buckwheat noodles. There is an infinite variety of ways to serve soba – sometimes in a soup, sometimes with a side dish for dipping.
Sashimi	Slices of raw fish served with wasabi (Japanese horse radish) and dipped

A1

in soy sauce. In some areas, whale
meat and horse meat are also served
in this way.

Sushi	Probably the most well-known Japanese cuisine. Small pieces of fish or seafood served on a bed of "sour" rice with wasabi and dipped in soy sauce. Prices range from the modest (usually where the customer selects pre-prepared dishes from a rotating conveyor belt) to the expensive, where a master chef will prepare each piece to order in front of the customer. In the top sushi restaurants it is often best to let the Master select what is freshest and most tasty.
Tako yaki	Small pieces of octopus, battered and grilled. Often served with pickled ginger.
Tempura	Battered and deep fried seafood, fish and vegetables served with a dipping sauce and grated daikon (Japanese radish). Said to have been introduced by the Portuguese.
Tonkatsu	Breaded and deep fried cuts of pork served with a special pungent sauce and shredded cabbage. Tonkatsu restaurants will usually also offer deep fried prawns and (in season) oysters.
Teppanyakai	Grilled meats and seafood prepared and sliced in front of the customer.
Udon	Flour based noodles usually served in a soup with a variety of toppings.
Unagi don	Broiled eel with a rich sauce served on a bed of rice. This dish is popular in the hot summer as it is thought to boost energy.
Yakisoba	Fried soba noodles with pork and vegetables usually served with picked ginger.
Yakitori	Skewers of chicken grilled over charcoal.

A1

Hotels

Japan's major cities boast a variety of hotels to suit most business travellers' budgets. There are any number of so-called "business hotels" which offer a simple but adequate no-frills service and – certainly in Tokyo and Osaka – there are international hotels of the very highest standard. A limited listing appears below but your travel agent should be able to advise on seasonal offers and other special deals that can cut down on the cost of a stay. The business traveller who is planning an extended stay might want to consider a serviced apartment as an alternative to a hotel. Oakwood is a highly respected name in this field, with a variety of residences available at varying prices. See http://www.oakwood.com/serviced-apartments/international/JP/212/Tokyo.html

If your business schedule allows you a little time for sight-seeing, a one- or two-night stay in a traditional Japanese inn (ryokan) is highly recommended. You will sleep in futon on a tatami-matted floor, be served the very finest local and seasonal cuisine, and in many cases be invited to take advantage of the inn's hot-spring baths (onsen). If you are lucky, you will choose an inn with an outdoor hot spring (ryotenburo). To find out more about this essentially Japanese experience, please visit http://www.ryokan.or.jp/index_en.html.

Hotels in Tokyo

(Bear in mind that many of the hotels listed also have properties in Japan's other major cities)

ANA Intercontinental   Tel: 03-3505-1111
            website: www.anaintercontinental-tokyo.jp/e/

The Conrad Tokyo   Tel: 03-6388 8000
                                            Website:
http://conradhotels1.hilton.com/en/ch/hotels/index.do?cty
                                         hocn=TYOCICI

The Grand Hyatt   Tel: 03-4333-1234
                    Website: tokyo.grand.hyatt.com

The Hilton Tokyo   Tel: 03-3344-5511
                                            Website:
        http://www1.hilton.com/en_US/hi/hotel/TYOHITW-
                          Hilton-Tokyo-hotel/index.do

A1

The Imperial Hotel   Tel: 03-3504-1111
Website: http://www.imperialhotel.co.jp/index_e.html

The New Otani Tokyo   Tel: 03-3265-1111
Website: http://www.newotani.co.jp/en/tokyo/

The Mandarin Oriental   Tel: 03-3270-8870
Website: http://www.mandarinoriental.com/tokyo/

The Okura   Tel: 03-3582-0111
Website: http://www.okura.com/tokyo/

The Park Hyatt   Tel: 03-5322-1234
Website:
http://www.tokyo.park.hyatt.com/hyatt/hotels/index.jsp3
45322 1234

The Peninsula   Tel: 03-6270-2888
Website:
http://www.peninsula.com/tokyo/en/default.aspx

The Ritz Carlton   Tel: 03-3423-8000
Website:
http://www.ritzcarlton.com/en/Properties/Tokyo/Default.
htm

The Westin Tokyo   Tel: 03-5423-7000
Website:
www.starwoodhotels.com/westin/property/overview/inde
x.html?propertyID=1062 - 63k -

A1

National holidays

Several days throughout the calendar year are designated
as national holidays. Banks, public offices and some
companies close on these days and it is best to avoid
trying to make business appointments. When a national
holiday falls on a weekend, the following Monday is
generally treated as the holiday. The April-May holidays
constitute what has become known as "Golden Week"
and many people take advantage of the string of holidays,
tagging on the intervening non-holidays so as to achieve
a block of time during which to take vacations either
domestically or overseas. Additionally, there is a period
in mid August tied to the Buddhist O-bon Festival when
traditionally the spirits of the deceased return to their
homes. Many people use this period to leave the cities

and return to their hometowns. The year end holiday, known as o-shogatsu, is perhaps the most important of all and though only January 1st is a designated national holiday it is not uncommon for businesses to remain closed for some days afterwards.

Date	Holiday
January 1st	New Year (*o-shogatsu*)
January – *second Monday of*	Coming of Age Day (*seijin no hi*)
February 11th	National Foundation Day (*kenkoku kinenbi*)
March 20th approx	Spring Equinox (*shunbun no hi*)
April 29th	Showa Day (*Showa no hi*) – the birthday of the former Emperor
May 3rd	Constitution Day (*kenpo kinenbi*)
May 4th	Greenery Day (*midori no hi*)
May 5th	Children's Day (*kodomo no hi*)
July – *third Monday of*	Ocean Day (*umi no hi*)
September – *third Monday of*	Respect for the Aged Day (*keiro no hi*)
September 23rd approx	Autumn Equinox (*shubun no hi*)
October – *second Monday of*	Health & Sports Day (*taiiku no hi*)
November 3rd	Culture Day (*bunka no hi*)
November 23rd	Labour Thanksgiving (*kinro kansha no hi*)
December 23rd	Emperor's Birthday (*tenno no tanjobi*)

A1

Religion

It is fair to say that religion per se does not play a great part in the lives of the Japanese, most of whom – if they had to – would describe themselves as Shintoists or Buddhists or both. Certainly most Japanese will encounter both belief systems: weddings are generally conducted according to Shinto rites, funerals according to Buddhist rituals.

Shinto (which is often translated as "the way of the gods") is Japan's native religion and until the occupation following World War II, was the state religion. It is both polytheistic (in other words there is no single deity) and animistic (the gods – known as *kami* – can be present in animals, plants, mountains, rivers, whatever). The gods reside in shrines and many of Japan's most celebrated festivals are associated with these.

Buddhism made its way from India through China and Korea in the 6th century and seems to have quickly found an accommodation with Shintoism so that before long the Buddhist monasteries were able to exert considerable political pressure (see Chapter One).

It may be helpful to understand that the teachings of the philosopher Kong Fu Zi (also known as Confucius) had a big impact on Japan in the Tokugawa Period. That influence is still apparent today in the importance the Japanese attach to loyalty, ethics and consideration for the individual.

A1

Christianity was introduced to Japan in 1542 by Portuguese missionaries and initially large numbers of people in Western Japan were converted. But the authorities, disturbed by such a strong influence from outside the country soon moved to stop the spread of the religion. Christians were severely persecuted and believers were forced underground (the so-called "hidden Christians" about which Shusaku Endo wrote so movingly in his novel "Silence"). By the mid 17th century Christianity had been all but eliminated and it was not until the mid-19th century Meiji Restoration that religious freedom was permitted. Even today, fewer than 1% of Japanese are Christians.

appendix two

appendix two